MORE LIKE THE MASTER

MORE LIKE THE
MASTER

a christian musician's reader

Edited by
Patrick Peterson &
Jane Hertenstein

Cornerstone Press Chicago
Chicago, Illinois

For further information, contact
        Cornerstone Press Chicago
        939 W. Wilson Ave.
        Chicago, IL 60640

ISBN 0-940895-25-0
99 98 97 96   4 3 2 1
Printed in the United States of America
Cover and interior designed by Pat Peterson/wheatsdesign
Cover photo by Thomas Wray. Used by permission

Library of Congress Cataloging-in-Publication Data

More like the Master : a Christian musician's reader
     p.   cm.
  Includes bibliographical references and index.
  ISBN 0-940895-25-0
  1. Ministers of music.   2. Contemporary Christian music-
-Vocational guidance.   I. Peterson, Patrick J.   II. Hertenstein, Jane.
ML3001.M865   1996
246'.7--dc20   96-22948
                                               CIP
                                            MN

contents

Introduction

Musicians need all the help they can get; I know, I am one. You get into music (or music gets into you) because you have something to say, or because it just feels good to play, or you're intrigued by the lifestyle—there are almost as many reasons as there are musicians.

If you're just starting, or if you have been around the music scene for a while, you probably still have more questions than answers as to *why* you're doing this. And there are certainly questions about working (or not working) with labels, trying to juggle practice time, touring, and family needs, all the while remaining true to your calling as a Christian. Though none of our authors claim to have all the answers, each struggled with similar issues and writes from their experience and hard-earned wisdom.

We have tried to touch on basic issues in this volume. In the back are references for further reading, and we hope to add to this collection in the future; think of *More Like the Master* as "volume one in a continuing series."

Many of these chapters have appeared in print previously as articles or booklets. Each piece has been edited to be consistent with our house stylebook the (naturally) *Chicago Manual of Style;* part of this was changing from British to American spelling where necessary.

I would like to thank each of the authors for their willingness to participate in this venture. And if you are just entering this wide and wild world of music—or are licking a few wounds received within "the business"—don't be afraid to ask questions whenever and wherever you can. There are many music veterans who are more than willing to help; they were once where you are now!

PAT PETERSON
Cornerstone Press Chicago

Acknowledgements

Begbie, Jeremy, "Music In God's Purposes" © 1989 Jeremy Begbie. Reprinted with permission of Jeremy Begbie and The Handsel Press, Ltd.

Card, Michael, "For God Alone" originally published in *CCM,* Vol. 18, No. 11, May 1996. © 1996 CCM Communications. Reprinted with permission.

Hakanson-Stacy, Michael, "The Practical Side of Independents" © 1996 Michael Hakanson-Stacy.

Kaiser, Glenn, "Finding the Balance" previously appeared as "Chatting With Glenn Kaiser" in *Reality,* Vol. 2, No. 9, June/July 1995. © The Bible College of New Zealand, Inc. 1995. Used by permission of *Reality.*

Kaiser, Glenn, "Talking Straight" previously appeared as "Talkin' Straight" in *CrossRhythms,* Issue 30. © 1995 *CrossRhythms.* Reprinted with permission of *CrossRhythms* and Glenn Kaiser.

Krist, Jan, "A Singing Life" © 1996 Jan Krist.

Talking Straight

Glenn Kaiser

Glenn is a twenty-five-year veteran of the contemporary Christian music scene, performing solo on the All My Days *worship project, teaming up with Darrell Mansfield and Larry Howard for blues sets, and contributing as lead vocalist for Resurrection Band. Glenn and his wife, Wendi, travel all over the world giving seminars on worship and God's central place in our lives. Glenn is currently a pastor at Jesus People USA Covenant Church in the inner-city of Chicago.*

First appeared in *CrossRhythms*. For more information on *CrossRhythms* contact the editors at *CrossRhythms,* P.O. Box 183, Plymouth PL3 4YN England.

I have few illusions about the possibility of a utopian society. I have lived in intentional Christian community for nearly twenty-five years and any thoughts of "perfect" anything–other than God himself–have long been forsaken!

In fact, the American thinker and essayist Henry David Thoreau only lasted about two years in his utopia. Interestingly, I have never heard anyone ask, "If life in the cabin on Walden Pond was as wonderful as he had us believing it was, why did he leave and never return to it?"

I love living in Christian community, (Jesus People USA, Chicago) common purse, inner-city crime, rubbish in the streets, hurting people, and all the rest. At the same time, I have never thought God called all believers to the exact lifestyle He called me to.

Having said all of this, I would ask the reader to think about the following opinion (mine): though industry and ministry are not absolutely incompatible, all of us lean toward one of the two.

As I have heard (and lived) horror stories about such problems as poor business practices, injustice, outright scams and various ongoing sins in the Christian music scene here in the land of plenty, I look to Jesus and his word for solutions. And I continually find myself thinking about one of the absolute root causes of these and most problems. This cancer is found in all of us. It is *self.*

Self indicates many (most?) of the far-reaching decisions made at executive levels in the business of the contemporary

Christian music industry. Consider this: unless you live in the Third World situation–as an artist, manager, agent, recording company exec, sales rep, or shopkeeper, you *choose* a basic standard of living. You seek to attain a particular set of living conditions. So you hire and fire, largely based on the i$$ue of the "bottom line."

The scope of this article does not allow me to unload reams of firsthand knowledge (not gossip, rumor or innuendo) of how a wife and her children are affected when a "Christian" label drops her husband . . . solely on the basis of sales. Did someone say, "ministry?" This, dear friends, is commerce.

Either the execs, board members, or stockholders decides that "X" amount of money must be made, cash flow attained and such. In terms of a company, no money means no business *or* ministry. Growth is a normal and acceptable goal. Stability has everything to do with good stewardship practices for the Christian businessman. I both understand and support this concept.

But next come the choices. How does one decide the appropriate car to drive, house to rent or buy, clothes to wear, leisure activities to pursue? At what point do riches, worries and lust for other things enter in and choke the fruit of the Word out of Christian music?

I have neither the right nor desire to propose a specific lifestyle approach to others. Community is a calling and a personal choice I have followed. Not all Christians will or should live exactly as I do. In fact, the Bible itself is silent when it comes to such specific guidelines. But what it does say is illuminating:

> "And the congregation of those who believed were of one heart and one soul; and not one (of them) claimed that anything belonging to him was his own but all things were common property to them. And with great power the apostles were giving witness to the resurrection of the Lord Jesus, and abundant grace was upon them all. For there was not a needy person among them, for all who were owners of land or houses would sell them and bring the proceeds of the sales, and lay them at the apostles' feet; and they would be distributed to each, as any had need." (Acts 4:32–35)

I know (and have known) quite a few people in Christian music. There are certainly artists who are gifted reprobates. There are also music industry businessmen who are truly regenerate, and live simple lifestyles for the sake of a lost world and a Church in need of teaching and admonishing. But it has been my experience that few artists drive BMWs and very few in the exec sphere drive cheapos. Few artists own their own homes, and fewer still seem to care. Per capita, I'd say the lion's share of the loot is being put into lifestyles that would certainly be called comfortable–and I'm not referring to the artists.

And I admit this as well: I am comfortable with a lot less than most, and am not in the very typical financial bind that most Christian artists find themselves in. What I do musically is sponsored by a sustained church body that simply supports its ministers and missions. In other words, I'm well aware that

I'm blessed. I am also not suggesting that Resurrection Band nor Glenn Kaiser have been brutalized by a corrupt Christian music industry. Most of the foolishness of the CCM industry has not and will not affect us directly.

But this is *not* the case for ninty-nine percent of the Christian artists I know. It is for them and their families that I am becoming more vocal as I grow older. I am convinced it is time to write publicly about the core diseases that have infected the Christian music industry.

May God help us to pray, speak out when and however necessary, and to model lives of commitment, sacrifice, and integrity to a church and a world in dire need of all three. If love and minisry is truly our aim, the target is certainly large enough to hit!

If the Kingdom of God is what Christian music is truly about, the kingdom of self will have to go. If by "ministry" we mean "service," perhaps our individual comfort quotients will have to be surrended to the Lordship of Christ along with everything else. Without such changes, a solvent "industry" may one day be all we have left.

As always, the Lord has the last word:

" . . . follow the impulses of your heart and the desires of your eyes. Yet know that God will bring you to judgment for all these things." (Eccles. 11:9)

"Love does no wrong to a neighbor; love therefore is the fulfillment of (the) law." (Rom. 13:10)

The Seven Deadly Sins of Contemporary Christian Music

Dwight Ozard

Dwight Ozard is the editor of Prism *magazine, the national publication of Evangelicals for Social Action. He hails from London, Ontario, Canada where at one time he served as the minister of youth at the Metropolitan United Church, Canada's largest mainline Protestant congregation. Over the last ten years, Dwight has been involved in Jesus music as a radio host-producer, concert promoter, and as a freelance writer. He now lives in Philadelphia, Penn., with his wife, Sheri Blick Ozard.*

Originally appeared in *Prism*. For more information on ESA or *Prism* please write the offices at ESA, 10 Lancaster Ave., Wynnewood, PA 19096.

We live in a world of great urgency and need, of overwhelming concern and brokenness. It is a world that desperately needs to see and know mercy and justice. Almost every day, we at Evangelicals for Social Action hear story after story that only serve to illustrate our world's inexhaustible need. Stories of fathers being forced at gunpoint to rape their daughters in Bosnia-Herzegovinia, stories of the immense suffering in Rwanda. Stories of the political and social turmoil in countries like Haiti. Stories of glaring and atrocious poverty and the problem of homelessness in our cities, of the rising toll of the abortion crisis, and the social collapse that fuels it, the rising costs and falling standards in health care and education. We see the continuing moral and spiritual collapse of our nation and, in many ways, feel powerless to address it.

We know very little except that it is a world that needs Jesus. That much is obvious. And in context of such desperate need, the reader of this volume is more than a little justified in wondering why in God's great name we're wasting so much paper discussing the arts. When the world is going to hell in a handbasket, do Christians, and indeed, does the world, need rock and roll?

I'll be honest with you. There was a time when I thought so, but I'm not so sure anymore. As I grew up through the '60s I watched two seemingly inseparable entities blossom to maturity side by side. On one hand, my child's eyes saw a growing awareness that things were not well with my world.

Every day, I saw signs of it, the biggest of which were the kids, just a few years older than I, in the streets. Angry and frustrated, they marched, yelled, swore, ranted and raged, and mostly, they sang. While a whole generation seemingly lost faith in the world, they found faith and hope in their music. Their loud, angry, rebellious, intemperate rock and roll was at once a rallying cry and the very thing around which they rallied, at once giving them voice when they had no other, and shaping that voice.

And like most kids my age, I grew up believing in the power of rock and roll. Despite all the anti-rock preaching I heard in my Pentecostal-Fundamentalist religious context (or perhaps because of it), by the time I was a teenager I had no doubt that music had the power to influence and change lives, and that a song could free the mind from old things, plant new ideas, soften or break the heart. I believed, because I experienced. For me, and for thousands of other kids like me, nothing came close—except maybe the swaying rhythm of the sweaty, tie-loosening evangelist at summer camp—to the spiritual, godly, enabling power, and the fear-inducing, gut-wrenching, heart-pounding power of rock and roll.

THE BIRTH OF "JESUS MUSIC"

We knew music could change the world, because it was changing us. And for those of us who were Christians, we knew that it could change the world for Jesus too. It was inevitable that the Jesus movement gave us "Jesus music"— contemporary Christian music— the radical revival's attempt to co-opt the powerful music of the counterculture. Larry Norman, Randy Matthews, Love Song, Mustard Seed Faith, Barry McGuire, and others began to define a whole new genre, a rock and roll that recaptured the spiritual roots the music had lost. And in the heady days of the Jesus movement, and those that followed, many of us believed that this would be a key tool to bring our generation to Christ.

But something happened along the way. Popular music in our secular culture stopped being the compelling force for change that it had become. While always profitable for the gangsters of corporate America, rock had been terrifying to them, nonetheless. Ed Sullivan insisted that lyrics be altered, pelvises be avoided, and songs be short. Despite the demand for songs of protest, radio managed to censor and ban the best of them, and for every anti-establishment song or group that forced its way into the popular consciousness, the establishment invented something—say a group like the Monkees—or capitalized on something—like a hairstyle or a dance—to deflect focus to the trivial. While I would not argue that the trivial didn't exist innately in rock music—it was, after all, a youth movement—I do believe that the brokers of its distribution handled it delicately and fearfully, aware of its explosive and disruptive power, and tried desperately to turn it into something less than threatening to the establishment.

And they succeeded. Playing on the counterculture's self-absorption and natural hedonism, (and its collective revolutionary exhaustion) corporate America not only helped mute pop music's subversive voice, they became an essential part of its voice. The danger associated with rock gave way to its immense profitability. Its rebel ends gave way to simple rebel posturing and bad hair; sex (to find free love) gave way to disco and one-night stands; drugs (as a way to enlightenment) gave way to cocaine to keep you intense; and (revolutionary) rock and roll gave way to corporate sponsorship of tours. All the form, all the fashion, and very little of the substance. Rock and roll, in just a few short years, went from a force that terrified our parents, preachers, and politicians, giving voice to our protests, threatening and mocking and exposing our false values and tearing down our institutions, to being the voice of the establishment, reinforcing our values, false and otherwise, and resisting institutional change. In short, as the Boomers grew up, sold out, and grew established, their music did too.

Two examples from recent pop history will suffice. Anyone who watched, in October of 1992, the "30th Anniversary Tribute to Bob Dylan" (arguably the most important protest singer-songwriter of the '60s and perhaps this century), could not avoid the painful irony of seeing Sinead O'Connor, regardless of how naive or misguided she might have been, being booed off the stage by a crowd angry with her now notorious ripping of the Pope's photo on "Saturday Night Live." It was, after all, an act of protest! That same fall, one of

Bill Clinton's key election strategies had been the courting of the MTV generation, through appearances on the Video network and Arsenio Hall. While 25 years earlier association with the rebellious rock generation would have been political suicide (remember Eugene McCarthy?), in 1992 it was essential to victory, a fact which is verified by Clinton's choice of which Ball to attend first on inauguration night—The MTV Ball.

With secular pop music rarely dangerous, contemporary Christian music thought itself ready to make a difference. But as it evolved against the backdrop of conservative evangelicalism, CCM was forced to defend its very existence, and its initial evangelical impulses—impulses rooted as much in the '60s counterculture that the Jesus movement left as in the new religion they embraced—were often eclipsed by its struggle to survive. As contemporary Christian music began to grow, we were bombarded with assaults from pastors and lecturers who were intent on showing CCM's evil, "pagan" (read: "jungle") roots. The debate against contemporary Christian music within the evangelical church, if nothing else, serves to illustrate just how much vestigial racism remained in its underbelly, with most of the arguments against "Christian rock" centering on the question of the "beat" and its alleged demonic and pagan roots. We were told that rock was "race music," and its syncopation was the front door to demonic possession and the backdoor to sexual promiscuity, sure to drive men and women into an orgiastic frenzy. Without rock and roll, we were assured, the "chaos" of the '60s would never have occurred, chaos that included, for most of the anti-rock preachers I heard and read, disruptive elements like the civil rights movement.

Mired in these debates, the focus of contemporary Christian music became its own legitimacy. CCM radio became a haven of inoffensive production, (with guitars and drums toned down as if to prove to the barons of evangelicalism that it wasn't really rock and roll), with lyrics designed explicitly to be so theologically and socially safe that the country's youth pastors could only hum along in bland approval. Contemporary Christian music quickly became, instead of an aggressive and relevant evangelistic tool, what can be best described as a soundtrack to the most mediocre of teen curricula, or worse, poorly conceived syncopated updates of our hymnody, designed to preserve our fading influence with our own. Even as popular music began to be embraced by the mainstream of the evangelical church, CCM continued its self-absorption (with some obvious and extraordinary exceptions), and became almost solely the realm of the evangelical subculture (not counter) that now supported it, irrelevant to most of those whom it originally hoped to reach.

This is best exemplified by two examples, one historical, the other personal. In the early '80s, several secular record companies began to take notice of the burgeoning contemporary Christian music industry (in 1981 CCM outsold both jazz and classical music), and either purchased or created their own "Christian" labels. Despite their marketing know-how and industry finesse, and even their lack of ethics, they were never able to really make a dint outside the evangelical world. The wave of "crossover" fever that accompanied this rush was over by 1987, and Christian labels began an even more rigorous policing of the "Christian" content of their artist's lyrics. The reality was that by 1985, contemporary Christian music had become its own world. Meanwhile, in my work as a youth minister and radio producer, I often tried to introduce youth to contemporary Christian music, especially those from churches outside of evangelicalism. Kids who were not initiated in the language of our subculture, and who were not immersed in its us-versus-them dualism almost always found contemporary Christian music to be at best silly, and at worst, deeply offensive.

With both its sociological and financial moorings in an easily offended religious ghetto, the imagined contemporary Christian music mission field became, all too quickly, simply the contemporary Christian music marketplace. And with that, many would argue, it died.

And so, for those of us disillusioned by the impotence of contemporary Christian music, the question becomes can contemporary Christian music be rescued—resurrected—from its demise? Can it be the force for conversion, for social change, for the radical calling of the Kingdom that it once envisioned itself to be? Can it be a relevant, engaging, transforming force in our culture?

I believe it can, but only if it faces its sins. It must face the sins that have at once made it a powerful force within the

Dwight Ozard

evangelical world and yet have kept it from relevancy, both within and outside of that community, and as art and as mission. It must face its sins, and begin to call the Church to do the same. For the reality is that its sins are the very sins of the evangelical culture that nurtured it into its deformed and irrelevant shape. What's wrong with contemporary Christian music is what's wrong with evangelicals. We have surrendered to *Sins of Misplaced Value, Marketplace Sins,* and *Spiritual Sin.*

Sins of Misplaced Value
    We have Equated Spirituality with Rhetoric
    We have Equated Holiness with Separation
    We have Embraced Technique over the Spirit
Sins of the Marketplace
    We have Spiritualized Commodity
    We have Commodified Spirituality
    We have Elevated Artist over Art (Celebritization)
Sins of the Spirit
    We have Fled the Cross

THE SINS OF MISPLACED VALUE

Growing up defensively in an atmosphere where its very survival hung on its ability to legitimate itself in the eyes of the Church, there is little surprise that contemporary Christian music became enamored with safety as quickly as it did. While its secular cousin could rail against the establishment quite freely (indeed, this was half of rock and roll's appeal), Christian rock had a more difficult time maintaining an anti-establishment stance. Besides, the criticism leveled at CCM called into question the legitimacy not just of their art, but their salvation as well.

Born out of revival fervor, and desperate for fellowship (and rightly so), the Jesus movement quickly adopted the popular theology of the one segment of the American religious establishment that embraced them: contemporary, "new" evangelism. This theology almost entirely dismissed the structural critique of the counterculture, and in so doing the Jesus movement accepted an agenda that for the most part hung on a narrow understanding of personal conversion that was replete with the separationist baggage of fundamentalism. Conversion was first a miracle of grace, yes. But it was one that demanded three specific evidences: a rigid and biblistic confessional orthodoxy; an understanding of personal holiness that was external, separatist, and easily verified; and evangelicalism's preoccupation with "results," a subtle emphasis on quantification that equated success with growth.

We have equated Spirituality with rhetoric

For the burgeoning contemporary Christian music industry, the legitimizing process began almost immediately. With the embrace of accepted evangelical rhetorical forms, and (for the most part) an abandonment of the social agenda that marked the counterculture, contemporary Christian music made itself (somewhat) acceptable to the evangelical world. There were of course, exceptions. Both Larry Norman and Randy Matthews, the founding fathers of CCM, filled their songs with the language of the street (remember "gonorrhea on Valentine's Day") and references to social issues, including homelessness, racism, and the war in Vietnam. Later, artists like Steve Taylor, Resurrection Band, and Mark Heard peppered their songs with social commentary. But as time progressed, and more and more money was made in contemporary Christian music, "issues" songs became exceedingly rare. By the mid-Eighties, the thematic narrowing of contemporary Christian music had become the rule, and those who veered from the accepted path simply were not played on the radio. The price was clear—make a living in Christian music, or sing about issues of conscience, justice, or even love. The business of CCM was not about these things.

This was complicated by the divergent and sometimes contradictory demands placed on contemporary Christian music by popular evangelicalism. The demands for holiness, understood by most as "separation from the world," seemed to predicate against using "worldly" music, a critique it met in CCM by its constant missionary posturing and its artistic reluctance. "All things to all men that some might be saved," they would quote, despite the fact that the "world" couldn't buy the music—it was sold almost exclusively through Christian bookstores.

This need not have resulted in the malaise that followed, save one thing: each of the demands, through time, were taken to unintended ends. The reality is that contemporary Christian music began not only demanding theological uniformity from its artists, but also that they address *only* theological themes. This began to happen in several ways. Contemporary Christian music that strayed outside the realm of the *overtly* spiritual (whether musically or lyrically) was questioned as "worldly." Artists were discouraged, both directly—by evangelical gatekeepers—and indirectly—through market forces—from writing about anything other than their "relationship with Christ," and musicians were discouraged from technical flare by leaders concerned that they might "indulge the flesh" and divert attention from Christ. (For example, Phil Keaggy's guitar heroics were discouraged by the Christian community in which he lived in the mid-seventies, while DeGarmo and Key's early flirtations with "positive pop" or "message music" were labeled as "compromising" the gospel message.) Fundamentalism's immensely unhealthy and unbiblical distinction between that which is sacred and secular—the kind of platonic dualism that divides everything into camps that has reached its zenith in artists like Carman and writers like Frank Perretti—was absorbed by CCM almost as soon as it became an industry. Only that which spoke directly and prosaically to the "spiritual" concerns of the Christian ghetto supporting it was regarded as "Christian"; that which didn't was suspect.

The irony of course, is that it is easy to write theologically correct songs, songs that use buzz words and hooks and enough "us versus them" rhetoric to make youth pastors take notice, tell their youth groups, and buy the records. Any deeper arbiter was forgotten. Theological formula became just that: a safe and easy passage to truth. Artists were discouraged from new takes on either their faith or experience of it. Eventually, and for the most part unintentionally, the new industry began to let two things happen. It began to let artists record for it without any real sense of or care for the depth of their faith, and it began to trust in technique and technology, rather than the authenticity of the artist's soul.

This was dangerous on several levels. First, it contributed to the further ghettoization of the Christian community. Instead of reaching out, contemporary Christian music withdrew from the world. Thus we perpetuated a vision of spirituality and discipleship that not only unsatisfactorily answered the questions that the world around us asks, but often ignored the questions altogether, insisting that they are suspect at best, or evil. Second, it limited the realm and growth of spiritual reflection and perpetuated a kind of evangelical neurosis. With only explicitly "spiritual" themes allowed on Christian radio, much of our life was seen as distinct from the spiritual, untouched by grace, despite the Spirit's obvious demands on those "unspiritual" areas. Our very humanity, for many young Christians raised in popular evangelical culture, became to be seen as a hindrance to faith. Third, it stymied critique.

Because of the evolution of an evangelical formulaic orthodoxy in contemporary Christian music, much of its initial reforming content was lost to the church, replaced by a series of "positive" messages that in reality simply affirmed our own "correctness." The artist, instead of being free to reflect and respond as a spiritual being was forced to write and perform as a "thing"—a kind of caricatured, cartoon cutout of what a Christian is, telling us what we already knew. And those who didn't play that game, were marginalized, vilified, or ignored.

It is plain that the prophets of the Old Testament—the artists, poets, performance artists, and songwriters of the Hebrew scriptures—faced those very same tensions. Over and over again, we hear the prophets being pressured by God's people to "Tell us good things. Tell us the right things. Tell us what we want to hear." What is also plain, is that contemporary Christian music as an industry, faced with these pressures, did just that.

But the call of the artist is neither to tell us what we want to hear, nor is it to tell us it in a form or way we like it, or makes us comfortable. It is simply to tell the truth, and tell it in a way that will force us to hear it.

And that demands new telling.

One of the great failures of our demands on contemporary Christian music, and on the artists themselves, has been our reverence for old symbols. Few of us have to be reminded of how powerless words can become when overused, or misused. Wonderful, potent metaphors like "born again" have almost completely lost their meaning outside (and at times within) our evangelical subculture. One of the artist's tasks is to help us find new metaphors and symbols (or recast the old ones in more potent forms), and thus help give them meaning. Instead of looking for ways to speak powerfully and freshly, we have simply re-said old things safely. And in doing so, we made the content of our art—the gospel itself, intersecting our lives—of no consequence. We have settled for cliché, the pedestrian, elevated the trivial, and created a pornography of the Spirit. We have done what God refused to do: we have made creation and the gospel something safe. By refusing to risk new visions and metaphors, by demanding that our art, and the art that we embrace, fit narrow formulae and patterns and comfortable visions, we have demanded an art that, instead of freeing truth, has confined it, and in turn, confined its hearers.

We have equated Holiness with Separation

Unfortunately, much of what passes as art in contemporary Christian music is about imposing meaning on our lives, or worse, is entirely distinct from them. Our concern with a holiness not rooted in relationship and love has led us on a journey to escape our experience, rather than find redemption in it. While this is in part a product of bad eschatology, it is also a precipitator of it. When we understand holiness as purity at the expense of or separation from something—be it either relationship, or creativity or reverence for creation or contact with it—it is inevitable that we will not only ghettoize our community, but our lives as well. Certain areas of our humanity become "off-limits" to our thinking and reflection. What is intended as a pursuit of purity becomes an escape from ourselves, or worse, our desire to show ourselves as better than the world.

So how does art pursue true holiness? Because holiness is about the Truth entering into our experience and transforming it, Christian art—including popular music—must be *world-ly,* earthly and earthy. It must be about life—all of life— even the parts we don't like. It will not avoid or seek escape from experience (whether that escape comes in ignoring or denial of parts of our humanity or in preoccupation with an other-worldly theology), but will instead embrace it, love it, and seek its redemption. And while this is in no way meant to excuse the Christian artist from the pursuit of purity, it ought to free us from the notion that there are certain subjects inappropriate for our art. What will distinguish us will not be what we examine, but the love that infuses our vision of it.

INCARNATION—EMBODYING TRUTH

There is no better theological foundation for this kind of theology of art than the incarnation of Christ Himself.[1] If the Creator would not stay outside of creation, than those of

1. If you need proof text, I suggest a new religion—but these references will help: John 1:1–14, Phil. 2:1–10; Col. 3:2, 3:12ff.

Dwight Ozard

us who would follow our Christ cannot seek to avoid it either, especially as we reflect on the meaning that Christ gives it. Whatever the nature of the purity we seek, it will be a purity in the midst of life.

And that is the call of the Christian, and specifically of the Christian artist. To illustrate, embrace, and incarnate our experience—our joy, pain, longings, failings, dreams, hopes, sexuality, spirituality—and seek its redemption. One writer has put it this way:

> What I'm suggesting is that art, outside the realm of human suffering, is not art. It's a counterfeit—shallow, oppressive, and senseless. But that doesn't imply that art's value is only as a vehicle. Art is more substantial than that. It's very content or substance is the human dilemma. And no canvas or lyric is finally born. We are constantly in process. . . .[2]

And that process demands that art, like true holiness, be an act of love, one that is willing to be soiled by association. And that process of incarnation is what gives art—music—the possibility of reaching beyond itself to the human soul.

We have embraced technique over the Spirit

There is further mystery yet. In following the incarnation, we follow a way that subverts the preoccupation with technique that our popular culture, and contemporary Christian music, has obsessed on. The way of Christ is the

2. Gordon Aeschliman, unpublished manuscript, with Tom Willett, "The Artist as Advocate."

renunciation of power, while the way of CCM (and most media ministries, and indeed, our entire Christian popular culture) is the manipulation of it. We have been so convinced as a culture that the "bread and circus" approach is what garnishes results that we have created a "pop" Christianity that actually despises simplicity and spontaneity. Listen to popular Christian radio, go to a concert, complete with pyrotechnic wonderment, or watch a modern worship band and tell me I'm wrong. We have learned to use our flair, formulae, and flash to get what we want from our audiences. Technology allows us to do that—create a substanceless wonderment and emotion in those we dazzle. Far too often, we manipulate and control our audiences so that no feeling or response is left to chance. What our firm orthodox formulations can't do, our flashpods, key changes, and amplification can.

Several years ago I used to do a seminar on rock music (I was for it) for churches and youth conferences. On occasion, I would begin the workshop with a time of worship, usually with a band. We would sing one song—first slowly, then building the tempo to a high level of energy, then pulling the band out for an a cappella turn. In the tradition I was working mostly in, this would lead to an extended period of (very) vocal worship. When we had finished, I would point to three members of the audience with whom I had met at random before the seminar began, and ask them to read the paper that I had given them. They would then read what I had told them would happen—an almost verbatim account of the worship just transpired. What the audience believed to be a very spontaneous moment I had, to a large degree, created. What to them *felt* like a pure moment of communication, was in reality a kind of manipulation.

My point was a simple—if brutal—one to make. Music (and art in general) can be exceptionally manipulative, and for the artist, the temptation is to rely on formulae, techniques, and devices that "produce," rather than to rely on the purity of the art itself. I clearly do not believe that all worship is manipulation (even in the contexts I manipulated). Nor am I a Ludditte. I do not believe that technology is *necessarily* a crutch for the artist—indeed, it is often an intricate component of the best art. But we must be aware of the manipulative dangers of technology, and careful to avoid them as we struggle to create faithfully.

The nature of creation and of art, as we have suggested, is the risk of being without power; it is about surrendering what we offer to the Spirit and to the listener. Christian artists ought to be most free in their expressions, because it is the Spirit that ultimately brings clarity, not their clever formulations. The abandonment of formula, separation, and technique ought to be liberating affirmations of the Spirit's work in our world, and through his people. Where we have failed to do so, we have failed to let the Spirit work.

But the sins of contemporary Christian music have not been simply ones of misplaced value. As contemporary Christian music grew up, it quickly became much more than just music: it became an industry. As it did so, it was tempted, and succumbed to three more sins that had long ago seduced the whole of the evangelical community.

THE SINS OF THE UNCHECKED MARKETPLACE

We Have Spiritualized Commodity

These sins flow out of the uncritical wedding of commerce and faith, and from the evolution of the Christian community into a subculture that embraced a majority of the assumptions of our society (rather than challenging them). In this atmosphere, the church can, and has, easily become a place where we are normal Americans, except with a quiet time, and we buy different stuff. The stuff we buy is sold to us, often by well-meaning sorts, but more often by people who have recognized the potential for profitability in our ghetto. Just as brewers have aimed specific products, say Colt 45, at specific demographics, so too have some entrepreneurs aimed their items at evangelicals. Often, the products not only meet a "felt need" of the community's, they also reinforce it. Thus, much of the music flowing out of contemporary Christian music not only speaks directly to evangelical prejudice, it reinforces it. Music is packaged not on its own merit, but as an alternative to the world's. While in light of Ozzy Osbourne's bat biting or Madonna's onstage auto-erotic escapades this doesn't seem like such bad a thing, its effect has been to create an artificially escalated worth for the alternative product, and to perpetuate a fundamentally flawed interpretation of the world (the extreme secular/sacred split). We are told it is good to buy and listen to this *thing* because *it* is Christian, and bad to buy or listen to this other *thing* because it isn't. In this context, bad art is passed off as good art, solely because of its worldview and sociological context, while good art is ignored or demonized for the same reason.

We Have Commodified Spirituality

Perhaps more insidious, Christian record companies are forced, by their own rhetoric, to pretend that they are more (or less) than what they are—companies, trying to make money— instead guising everything they do with the ruse of "ministry." This is not to suggest that ministry doesn't occur, but it is almost always secondary to the business of running a profitable company. The reality is, with few exceptions, when an artist is no longer profitable, she is dropped from a label, regardless of her ministry value, or spiritual depth. Spirituality, real or otherwise, has become a marketing ploy that is not sustained by the market's pressures. While young Christians are told they should buy a disc because it is by a "godly" artist— a step precariously close to simony—the company is under no compulsion to retain the artist for that reason.

Moreover, we need to recognize that often an artist is signed for reasons quite foreign to ministry concerns: name recognition, sound, or sex appeal. The element of celebrity in contemporary Christian music cannot be underestimated as a force for selling records—or as a destroyer of art and of ministry. Here again, CCM did what radio preachers, revivalists, and writers had been doing for years in the North American Christian context: milking recognition and notoriety for profit, advancement, and at times, for the Kingdom. While I would not argue that Christian art should be anonymous, there is something dissonant about getting a "Christian" autograph, or having a "star system" of artists who claim to follow the incarnate one, who was born in a barn and died on a trash heap.

This is true for two ironically related reasons. Christian celebrities, by definition, are held up as super-citizens of the Kingdom, and therefore are often either: a) immune from scrutiny, and therefore allowed to live as both Christians and artists with little or no accountability for their lives or ideas; or b) held to such rigid scrutiny that they are neither allowed to be human or to experiment as artists and Christians. Celebrity is a subtle (albeit prestigious and sometimes lucrative) kind of objectification that allows the church to mimic the world yet still pretend itself distinct.

TOWARD A CHRISTIAN AESTHETIC?

The notion of the incarnation demands our art abandon power, prestige, and the marketplace. What then, in our world, is left? One writer has said this:

> Some would say that if Christian music has any appropriate subject, it would be to communicate the concerns that were of primary importance to Jesus. . . . Would not music that calls itself "Christian" take us into the chamber of human travail? Why else would it be called "Christian?" If the incarnation has any significance, it seems to be the unarguable truth that the gospel is tethered to the human reality.[3]

But it is not enough to simply be about reality. Or even to embrace it. Art, especially Christian art, does not simply reproduce reality, but rather interprets it. It provides meaning. It sees life, and tries to make sense of it in a new way, and then gives it back to us to move us, and to be experienced again, through new eyes.

How does it do this?

It touches the heart, the soul, the center of our being. It speaks from great need to great need, and it refuses to be side-tracked from what is at our core, or be seduced by the immediacy of sensationalism or sentiment. It speaks to our mind, challenging and stretching us, speaking to our narrow, confining patterns of interpretation, and demanding they hear, see, and experience life in new ways, trying to make

3. Aeschliman, op. cit.

sense, and to find sense, even of and in non-sense. It brings creation, especially humanity, together, creating community, and reminding us of our common experience as humans created in God's image, on God's own earth. Finally, it calls us to action, to not only understand experience, but experience it, to leap into our world with abandon.

But what about the content of *meaning*? What should art say about our world, and experience of it? This I believe, leads us to the seventh sin of contemporary Christian music.

We have fled the Cross

We have sought, in our sheltered Christian experience, to flee suffering, and demanded that our art do likewise. We have sought a painless redemption, both of our souls and our world. And so our redemption has been incomplete, our art ineffectual, and our hope has been misplaced. Art, Christians believe, is fundamentally about creation—about sharing in God's image to reveal both His plan and Himself to us, to all of us and to the whole of us. But not creation alone—it is about interpreting creation through the eyes of the cross. As Reinhold Marxhausen, artist and former professor of art at Concordia College has said,

> It is the role of the artist to create new symbols, to show God to people in another way, to help them be aware of the world around them. The purpose of art is to make whole. The purpose of religion and redemption is to make whole.[4]

4. Interview, *The Door,* Issue 128, p. 13.

Because of this, the Incarnation did not flee suffering; in fact, it is incomplete without it. And that suffering is pointed and purposeful: it reveals the very heart and nature of God, and offers that God to the world. The ultimate meaning of our existence is found only here, at Calvary, or when Calvary is made real. Here our status as creatures at once desperately in need and desperately loved is made clearly known. Here we learn that in spite of our rebellion and the pain we have caused our Creator, he has neither abandoned us to our choices, nor has he left us. And here alone can the artist find the redemption that God seeks to reveal in our experience. It is here that Hope is found.

Because it is committed to the cross, it is the nature of *godly* art to risk. For God, the act of creation was a glorious, beautiful, and *dangerous* thing. It was dangerous because it was *free.* Yahweh risked being misunderstood, abused, rejected, distorted, all that He might reveal himself, redeem His creation and show His love. For this reason, Christian art will always be a reflection on our experience of that Person, that Truth, who has embraced us in the incarnation. Christian art is always about incarnation—*en-flesh-ment.*

In this light, Christian art will never be simply about the clever or beautiful arrangement of the right words or images. Art, like the Christian life, cannot be just about right ideas, formula, or proposition, to be *simply* repeated or claimed, affirmed or even understood. Art must arise from and be rooted in what is *real,* because art is fundamentally an exercise in interpreting our lives and the life around us. It must arise from wonder and hope and dreams of the transcendent, yes, but be always based in experience, flowing from and embracing the immanent. It is about finding meaning—hope—even in the bleakest of our lives.

What does that make the faithful artist, and indeed, the faithful Christian, then, in our world of false hopes and dreams? They are revolutionary. Their very existence challenges what has been, and threatens it with exposure and with transformation. The genuine artist is absolutely free (not from the rules of craft, but from the artificial restraints of formula or tradition), because they have encountered the great mystery of a Creator God that has never once forsaken His creation, indeed, who has leapt into it incarnately, who has promised to redeem it all, and has promised to redeem it through the gifts of His own people. The genuine artist is free to offer up what she fashions out of the stuff of her life, to both her God and her brothers and sisters, and free to trust God to make it meaningful. And the genuinely Christian artist is one who lives in the light of the Cross, offering not only their art, but their lives, to God as vehicles of mercy, grace, redemption, and meaning.

The task of the artist then is plainly a revolutionary one. One of subversion. To make way for the new humanity—the Kingdom—by supplanting the old and offering glimpses of the new in the stuff they create. It is here, in these frail offerings, that the Spirit dwells and moves and calls and dances and inspires, where the Spirit takes our weakness and makes it strength. When contemporary Christian music has transcended the status quo of our expectations and actually succeeded in touching, moving, challenging, and inspiring us, it has been when it has, in spite of all the baggage and sins of its context, done just that. And if it is to survive as anything other than a illegitimate and irrelevant child of American religion, it must reclaim its revolutionary, subversive, and incarnational calling.

High and Holy Calling

Charlie Peacock

Charlie Peacock is currently involved in re:think, *his own record label begun in November 1995. He is a prolific songwriter with several of his songs showing up on albums for Amy Grant, Margaret Becker, and Out of the Grey. Charlie has also produced albums for Out of the Grey, Margaret Becker, and Cheri Keaggy, winning a Dove Award for Producer of the Year in 1995. His current album project is titled* strangelanguage.

Previously appeared in the Art House newsletter, spring 1996. For more information on the Art House newsletter please write to the Art House, P.O. Box 210694, Nashville, TN 37221.

It is the Sixties, sometime between JFK and Haight-Ashbury. I'm just a child, one child among several seated in a classroom. There are four neat rows of desks with six desks to a row. Each desk, constructed of wood and steel, has a hole at the top for an inkwell. Since the universal conversion from ink to #2 pencils, the only activity the inkwell enjoys is the rush of gravity as a crumpled piece of paper or a wad of Bazooka drops from the hand of a student into the cavity of the desk. What pleasure.

I'm lucky. I have my pleasures, too. My desk is number four in the row next to the windows that look out onto Plumas Street. From my coveted position I have a reasonably unobstructed view of the front door of the corner store where I will most certainly purchase cinnamon toothpicks when the last bell rings and I am set free.

There are days, wistful days, when the autumn breeze dances through the open windows with such enticement and abandon that I cannot resist climbing aboard for a ride. Straddling the wind I hold on for life and carefully navigate the slender gap between the open window and its sill. Wide open space. I rocket the sky then fall and dart like the swallow. High above my little town I conclude there are more rich people in Yuba City than I had thought—so many swimming pools.

When I tire of flight I'm back in my seat, busy, shrinking. I make myself small enough to walk along the top of my teacher's desk. I climb onto the open pages of her gradebook and look for my name. I don't find it; I hear it.

Charlie Peacock

"Chuck, turn around in your seat and face the blackboard."

And with those words I'm brought back to size. I've been caught daydreaming. Again.

IMAGINATION AND CREATIVITY

Daydreaming is nothing like dreaming at night. When you daydream you're in control of your choices. You are free to imagine, and to imagine is to dive deep into an ocean of possibilities. Imagination is the power at work in us that allows us to make images. Not drawings or physical images, that's creativity—the fruit of imagining. Rather, when you think of the imagination, think of it as making images that initiate from, and remain within, the mind.

What can the imagination see with eyes closed? What can it construct without moving a finger? What can it taste though the tongue is locked up tight? Innumerable things, infinite images and choices, far more than we can describe or name. In truth, the sheer number of images the mind can imagine is so great that you or I could never think of nor catalog them all in a lifetime. The breadth, height, and depth of the imagination is never known in full by any one man or woman. Even with all her brilliance Dorothy Sayers did not possess what the Bible describes as the fullness of imagination. Neither did Da Vinci, Kepler, or Bach. It's too vast to be known in such a way. There is no one human mind that could possibly hold the collective imagination of history past, the present moment, and the history of imagination yet to be written. It is a feat beyond the finite human mind. It takes all of humanity to even begin to articulate something so grand. Each of us has an important role to play in contributing to the collective imagination of our time. Every contribution is important. There are no small roles.

Immeasurable acts of creativity are born out of the simplest of daydreams and imaginings. For centuries children had imagined the ability to fly like a bird or to shrink themselves so small as to travel in places where the human body could not go. Today in our time, we do fly, in rockets, jets, and gliders, and through laparoscopic surgery shrink small enough to travel inside the human body. How did this come to be? Someone went beyond the daydream to the tangible reality of these extraordinary inventions. They created. And what once did not exist, now exists.

Acts of creativity and invention are the fruits of the imagination. If the role of the imagination is to call forth images, then the role of creativity is to carry the image from the world of the imagination to the world of everyday life. One is responsible for dreams, the other is responsible for making dreams come true. One thinks, the other acts. The imagination is connected to a multiplicity of things that could be. Creativity is connected to a multiplicity of things that are.

GOD IS A CREATOR GOD

It is natural for Christians to focus on God the Redeemer. After all, redemption is something we have experienced and are experiencing daily in the Christian life. Focus on Christ is essential to the Christian life for it is Christ that makes us Christians. In Christ Jesus, God is making all things new. Alleluia. Our praise for such a glorious idea should never stop. Even so, before God began making all things new, God made all things.

In the beginning God created the heavens and the earth. (Gen. 1:1)

Through this scripture we encounter the Creator, the maker of all things. He is the origin of everything that has been made. He is the Author, the Inventor, the Artist. Max Lucado describes Him as a "tireless dreamer and designer."[1] This is an apt description, for God cannot tire of Himself. In Him dwells the fullness of imagination and He delights in using it. He absolutely loves being who He is—the Creator.

And God said, "Let there be light"; and there was light. (Gen. 1:3)

By His intelligence He imagined a universe, and by His divine utterance He created it. He is a God who thinks, speaks and acts. He is a knowable personal being who loves what He

1. Max Lucado, *In the Eye of the Storm* (Dalla, Tex.s: Word Publishing, 1995), 4.

has created. Because of this, He communicates with His creation, nurtures it and sustains it.

WE ARE MEN AND WOMEN CREATED IN THE IMAGE OF GOD

> Then God said, "Let Us make man in Our image, according to Our likeness; let them have dominion over the fish of the sea, over the birds of the air, and over the cattle, over all the earth and over every creeping thing that creeps on the earth." So God created man in His own image; in the image of God He created him; male and female He created them. (Gen. 1:26–27 NKJV)

While the world increasingly teaches and lives out its belief in the insignificance of the human, Christians teach that men and women are the most significant of all God's creation, since the privilege of being an image-bearer of God is given to them alone. To explain the image as being intrinsic to men and women would be incorrect. The image of God in humankind is extrinsic in that it has been imparted to us and imprinted on our being by the Creator. And for that reason alone it should be esteemed. In like manner, if we describe creativity and works of the imagination as being intrinsic to humanity, we are really describing the extrinsic. These good gifts have come from God and are a reflection of Him.

CREATED TO BE CREATIVE

Creativity is at the heart of our reflection of God's image. "In creating man God completes his activity and in obedience to God man continues God's creativity."[2] As image-bearers we are to mirror God's creativity. We are in truth created to be creators. We are to use our intelligence to think, to speak, and to act imaginatively and creatively. We are made, in a very real sense, to partner with God in continuing the process of creating the world and all that is in it. Our work is to flesh out the incredible creative potential of what God has created. God is the origin of everything, the true throne of originality belongs to Him alone. Only He can create out of nothing, because in Him, is the very power of being, what theologians call aseity or self-existence. When we make something new, something never seen before in history, we create out of what God has called into being. We are image-bearers, yet utterly dependent on the One whose image we bear, for in God we move and live and have our being.

DOMINION IS CREATIVE, MEANINGFUL WORK

God has given us meaningful work through which we use our imaginations and express our creativity. Creative work

2. George Carey, *I Believe In Man* (Grand Rapids, Mich.: Eerdmans, 1977), 32.

is connected to the idea of dominion or ruling. Dominion, introduced in Genesis 1:26–27, should not be confused with negative images of dominating. Rather, it is a role of caretaking, stewardship, and development. In giving man dominion, God appointed him governor over creation. As with any high office, there is accountability and responsibility. Humans are accountable to the Sovereign for the way in which they govern. For that reason God has equipped us to rule with love and wisdom, and we are not permitted to exploit creation for selfish purposes. To be anything but careful with what God has made is to mishandle His creativity. To mishandle His creativity is to misunderstand the seriousness of our role as his representatives on earth.

CREATED TO BE HOLY

The image of God in humankind involves a moral dimension as well as a creative dimension. We are like God in that we are moral beings. We possess reason and will and the ability to make choices and to follow through on those choices. We are to choose well and, by so doing, mirror God's holiness. Our choices are to be fueled by love and wisdom, just as God's are. We are to be holy as God is holy. The special dignity of being human, according to J. I. Packer, is that, "As humans, we may reflect and reproduce at our own creaturely level the holy ways of God, and thus act as his direct representatives on earth. This is what humans are made to do, and in one sense we are human only to the extent that we are doing it."[3]

Our humanness is made complete by living as God made us to live—as holy caretakers, imagining and creating to the benefit of everyone and everything under our care. This is the high and holy calling of the image-bearer.

3. J. I. Packer, *Concise Theology* (Wheaton: Tyndale House, 1993), 71.

A Singing Life

Jan Krist

Singer-songwriter Jan Krist's musical roots stretch back to the late 60s, and she has been astounding audiences in the Midwest for years. She has recorded two projects, Decapitated Society *in 1992 and* Wing and a Prayer *in 1993. She is currently finishing her third project,* Curious. *In 1993* Wing n a Prayer *was a Spotlight review in* Billboard *magazine (only the second time a recording on a Christian label was given that spot by* Billboard*).*

The porch was screened and the steps leading up were narrow and concrete. However, for a two-year-old it was an ample stage. My mother and sister sat in the grass and giggled at me, a red-haired, freckled faced singer, ". . . She wore an itsie-bitsie-teeny-weeny-yellow-polka-dot bikini." By the time I was seven I had advanced to standing on top of the dog house singing "Johnny Angel."

In 1968 I saw Amy Fong, a sophomore from Berkley High School sing "Suzanne" by Leonard Cohen at a talent show hosted by the junior high school I was attending. That was it. I got a guitar, mastered G C D F Em, and was writing my own songs as well as learning songs like "All Along the Watchtower" and "Early Morning Rain."

1969 was an amazing year for me. It was the year of my first guitar, my first date, my first performance, and my first composition. Nineteen sixty nine was also the apex of the Jesus Movement and it was the year I fell in love with Jesus. I began writing songs from a Christian perspective. The music I wrote contained within it the hope that had ignited me. It still does.

In 1973, a year after high school graduation, I married Tom Krist. I was eighteen years old. Within four months I was pregnant and at nineteen, I gave birth to my daughter Amon. Motherhood presented an incredible challenge. Amy demanded my time. She was beautiful, fascinating, tyrannical. My artistic drive, like my child, was also loud and demanding. I couldn't avoid it. So I would sandwich it in. I found the best time to work was late at night, but even that wasn't easy

Jan Krist

because Amy didn't like to sleep much.

In 1976 we moved into a Christian "household" with four other musicians. We wanted to be part of urban renewal. Tom and I put the house and bills in our name. It was a disaster.

Two of the members of our household became unemployed. Within a short time they had run up significant phone bills, and having no money or prospects decided to move out. We were left with their unpaid bills.

We needed some extra income to deal with the bills that we had inherited from our failed attempt at small-scale communal living. So I started playing in bars, the only paying venue open to local musicians. I could leave after Amy was in bed, make $50 or $60 and be home in time to get four or five hours of sleep before Amy woke up. I didn't have to miss a minute of my child's day and yet I could make enough money to help get us through the month.

I started out as part of a duo. Paul Irwin, my guitarist, and I auditioned and began gigging in clubs around Detroit. One week Paul went to see his family in Chicago. We had a gig that Friday night. He called me Friday at 5:00 P.M. He had decided he wasn't coming back to Detroit. Bang! I was solo. I had to work harder at my skills to make it working the clubs, but I learned a lot.

Tom, Amy, and I moved into an apartment in Royal Oak, a northern suburb of Detroit. I taught guitar one day a week and did gigs five or six nights a week. I played anywhere I could get a gig. I even played on a bus to Toledo! My friends promoted my music and shared bootleg recordings of concerts with other people. As a result, my music found its way to some record companies in Nashville.

A recording label sent plane tickets so I could come down to audition. Tom and I stayed with an A & R man for the weekend and I sang all of my songs in his living room. On Sunday afternoon as we were packing he said, "Jan, I love your music. My concern, though, is that it's not commercial enough." He handed me a copy of Amy Grant's first record, fresh off the press. "Take this home. Study the writing. See if you can write a little more like this. Then I think we can work."

I returned home, I listened, and wondered why I, at twenty-four-years-old, was being coached to write and sing like a sixteen-year-old. I wondered why would they want another Amy Grant. She was already doing a splendid job of being herself. I wanted to do something original, my own, and not recycle someone else's style. As a child of the Creator, I believed strongly that we each held our own creative spark.

Meanwhile, back at home things weren't going too well. In the five years that Tom and I had been married, we had lived in four homes. Tom had worked at three different jobs and was looking for new employment again. His dreams were my nightmares. He dreamed of quitting work altogether and riding across the country or sailing around the world. I needed a routine in normal surroundings. We were so different. We were constantly finding ourselves at an impasse, and yet as Christians, we wanted to find a common place where our marriage could not only exist, but thrive.

We attended a charismatic church that had broken off from a very fundamental church. The church leaders were experimenting with the concept of "shepherding." We needed some guidance to get through the difficulties that overwhelmed us and this looked like the answer.

We went to the elders for counseling. After much prayer, they came back to us and told us that they believed the possibility of a recording contract for me was too much of a distraction for Tom. "He doesn't know what he wants to do, and as the man of the house, he needs to focus on becoming the spiritual leader and the head of the household. He needs to stop putting off making his own career move because of you." They asked me to support him within his role as husband and provider. They told me that they believed it was "God's leading" that I lay down my gift for now at least. "Let God decide if you should ever pick it up again, and if so, how."

They advised us to move closer to the community (which brought us back to Detroit). Tom was told to sit tight at the job he was at until some things fell together. If I had been a man would they have asked me to walk away from my music? Would they have asked my wife to support "the call put on my life?"

I went along with my church's advice. I supported my husband in his search for a professional direction. I dropped out of the creative "scene," and directed my energies towards my roles as wife and mother. We moved into Detroit to be close to the fellowship. I worked with the church and organized drivers to take a Vietnamese family to their doctor appointments, to the grocery store, etc. I volunteered to clean house for a woman from my church who was too ill to take care of her home.

I had my second child, Ian. We put Amon in a private kindergarten. I stayed busy, and mourned the loss of the interaction and artistry I had rehearsed for my whole life. I had been given a gift and now it was buried.

"After all," I mused, "playing in bars wasn't the pinnacle of my musical aspirations, and I knew the Christian music realm didn't want my music. I wasn't about to change my writing to become commercial enough for mass consumption. Anyway, I didn't think it was my musical style that needed to change.

It burdened my soul to think of letting go of something I cared about as passionately as my music, and it troubled Tom to see me do it. My prayer was that if the elders were wrong, God would somehow, in the greater cosmic scope of things, see my heart, forgive us all, and set things right.

A TIME TO BUILD, A TIME TO BREAK DOWN

At some point I began to write again. I couldn't suppress the urge; I could no longer bury my talent. My creative juices were like a stopped up spring slowly building up pressure, trying to get out. I had to write, I had to sing.

In August of 1984 our third child, orange-haired Michael, was born. We moved back to the suburbs and bought a house which we gutted, and worked on every day for three years.

Sundays became the most important work day as we labored under time constraints. There was pressure to bring the house up to code and refinance it, paying off the land contract. We fought, we made up, we left our church and neglected to find another one.

The years passed and we were constantly stressed, constantly at odds with one another. We played tug of war over the pay check between paying bills and buying materials. To try and catch us up, I went back to singing in bars.

In the 80's, playing in bars was a bit like rearranging deck chairs on the Titanic. Original music was out. Musicians were encouraged to use sequenced music along with their guitars to duplicate the hits of the last four decades, and "play it again." I didn't sink so low as to play canned music, but I did sing "Margaritaville." I played in a duo, a trio, and solo. I would make it home at three or four in the morning and get up at seven to get the kids off to school.

As the 90's rolled into view, I found myself in the driest place I have ever been. My emotional energy was drained. Writing and performing had been a type of therapy for me. Now creativity was set aside and music became utilitarian, passion fell prey to practicality.

Fewer bars were hiring musicians; I was working less while our bill pile was growing. Stress was a cottage industry with us. It seemed there were always too many plates in the air and too few hands to keep them from tumbling down around us.

While I was determined not to repeat the mistakes of my

father (who was an alcoholic) or mother (and her struggles with codependency), I had done little to resolve the issues troubling me. I tried to smooth things over and provide a peaceful home for my family. "Don't rock the boat" was tattooed on my brain cells. But it was time for me to stop managing the emotions of the people around me. It was time to stop trying to single-handedly save us from every catastrophe. During this time I realized that my faith was not separate from my music such as cream floating to the top of a bottle of milk. Christianity was homogeneous in my life. I realized art was meant to be an honest exchange, and a true reflection of the life I was living. The struggle of faith.

My depression wasn't something for which I blame someone else. I needed to go back to church and take the kids with me. I searched for a new church, but Tom didn't like any of the ones I found. So we decided to go back to our old church in Detroit which had evolved into a Vineyard Christian Fellowship. Mostly I attended alone with the kids.

I became a part-time nursery school teacher. Michael was in kindergarten and my work schedule coincided with his school hours. I started a band, Zookini Opera, and stopped worrying about the number of gigs disappearing in the area.

In 1992, Tom and I had a breakthrough in our finances. It was time for me to put my music on tape. I recorded *Decapitated Society* at Sky Studio in Swartz Creek, Michigan. The guys in the band were not happy that I was doing a solo project, but Tom wasn't willing to finance a band project.

As I finished the recording, I got a call from a friend who was shopping for projects to lease for a new label. I sent him a tape, signed with the label, and my music was propelled into a life of its own. But the rest of my world disintegrated. Stresses that had kept things on rocky ground for twenty years, finally wrenched us apart. We had been in counseling for almost two years, both together and individually, but the situation was only getting worse.

The trouble in our marriage came to a head, and I found myself wishing I had never been born. My desire to obey the biblical commands concerning marriage and divorce was challenged by the reality I found myself in. I filed for divorce.

Now I had to find a way to support the kids and myself. I needed to work a full-time job that provided health benefits, but I had no job training. I couldn't get a job that paid enough to support my family. My stilted musical career didn't provide enough to support us and purchase insurance. I had to work two jobs to care for my children. The music took on the bulky inconvenience of a family business. It required not only my time, it required my kids' as well. They had to travel with me, help me sell product, and stay up until all hours of the night.

I was never good at business; it was time to let someone else argue out the business side of music for me and I hired a manager. The business side of music I discovered was like the business side of a horse. It was dangerous for a novice.

After my divorce, I went back into the studio and recorded my second project, *Wing and a Prayer*. I co-produced *Wing* with my old friend Paul Irwin. The recording was received enthusiastically by the critical community. I was given a Spotlight review in *Billboard* magazine, it was only the second time in the history of *Billboard* that a recording with Christian affiliations had been given that honor.

But the tension between art and business was eclipsed by my need to provide for my family. I began a new round of playing clubs and again looked at the idea of a 9 to 5 job. I took a full-time position with benefits at an assisted-living facility for senior citizens. I worked there for two years and toured two weekends a month.

In 1994 I took the summer off to record demos, write, and tour. In the fall, though, my boys came back from visiting their dad and I needed steady work again. I took a job with a paint crew. We painted outside until the weather kicked us in. Then I did apartments and house interiors.

By February of 1995 work was taking its toll. I realized something was terribly wrong while driving back from a gig in Chicago. I was exhausted and worried; coffee wasn't putting a dent in my drag. I was leaving work by 2 P.M. to come home and sleep; it was difficult getting through the day. After tests, my doctor said a mono virus which had laid dormant in my body for twenty-five years had reactivated. He was reluctant to call it chronic fatigue syndrome, he called it fatigue. He recommended a vegetarian diet and sent me on my way.

I couldn't paint apartments anymore. I went back to working with seniors. The facility was brand new and had zero residents for the first two months I worked there. Thankfully, as the number of residents increased, so did my energy level. I still have to be careful, but I'm much better.

THE TIDE CHANGES

In July 1995, I married Alan Finkbeiner, a fellow musician. We share the same love for music except he reveals his passion in strange ways. He beats on tables, steering wheels, and furniture. He taps his fingers in rhythmic patterns on my back when he hugs me. He's a drummer.

When our art becomes a career, it can be good and bad. On the good side, these works of ours can become satellites. They go farther and faster than we ever could take them on our own. They can also motivate us to produce a greater volume of work when we see an outlet for our art.

On the down side, when our art becomes a career it may need to be a second job, because even good artists and musicians have difficulty finding enough work to bring home the Bacos. And, should our art become an industry, we may find our satellite broadcasting a hybrid version of our art, or we may have to deal with our satellite colliding with the world of commerce and crashing to the earth.

For me artistic expression has to reflect the collision of faith and humanity, idealism and reality, devastation and hope. I have always been an artist. My art has not always been a product. Those of us who are artists, would be artists whether we sang our songs to the dog or hung our paintings in the kitchen. It's what we do. It's who we are.

I began to pursue a career in music when I started playing bars. I began a career as an artist in 1992 when I recorded *Decapitated Society*. Since then I have recorded *Wing and a Prayer* and *Curious*. I was a finalist in 1992 at the Kerrville Songwriting competition in Kerrville, Texas. In 1996 I was given an award by the *Detroit News* and *Metro Times* for best vocalist in acoustic music in Detroit.

Sometimes people ask why it's taken me so long to get started on my career. Life is a strange mix of artistic impulses and practical concerns. I have tried to base my decisions on what I thought would work for my family. The business of music had to take a back seat to my family's needs.

We need to continue to develop as artists throughout the course of our lives. We're never too young to start, never too old to start over.

I've been doing music since I was old enough to coo. I want to do the best art I can so I push myself to do more, do better. It's what I do, who God made me to be. It is the passion that God has given me to do this that drives me on. It energizes me in the middle of the night as I search my thesaurus for one more option before committing to a lyric. It is the passion seed planted in the soul of that two-year-old bopping her knees and singing to her sister and mom from the front porch steps.

For God Alone

Michael Card

Michael Card is a talented and respected musician. With a master's degree in biblical studies, Michael draws from God's word not only for his lyrics, but also for several award winning books. Sleep Sound in Jesus *was nominated for a C. S. Lewis Children's Book Award and* Immanuel: Reflections on the Life of Christ *was a finalist for a Gold Medallion Book Award. His latest book is* Parable of Joy: Reflections on the Wisdom from the Book of John. *His current album is* Poiema.

Originally published in the May 1996 issue of *CCM* magazine. For information about *CCM*, please call (800) 333-9643.

For some years now a question has increasingly reared its head. It is whispered with awe as if it were some great dilemma, as if the answer might be some deep paradoxical mystery. It has many forms and can be asked in a number of ways: "How does fame fit in to CCM?" "Does an artist need to be more famous to have a better ministry?" "Should an artist want to be a celebrity?"

I have been asked to comment on this deep dark conundrum, to share some of my vast wisdom on the subject, since I've been a part of CCM for about 15 years now. But the truth is, I am qualified to answer the question (and I believe there most certainly is an answer) only insofar as I have struggled with, and for the most part lost, in the battle of pride and ego. The only real personal victories have been won in community with brothers like Phil Keaggy, Steve Green, and Wes King.

The philosopher Kierkegaard said, "Life must be lived forward, but it can only be understood backwards." Though I've never felt like a celebrity (and my wife, Susan, assures me that I am not), I have received a good deal more attention and yes, even fame, than I've deserved in the forward motion of my life. But every time I take a backwards look on my years in the spotlight, I see clearly what Malcolm Muggeridge called the "sheer fantasy of fame." From this vantage point even the little recognition I've received turns out to be "wood, hay and stubble."

The truth is, it is not in the smallness of my life that we can ever hope to find the answer but only in the infinitely deep and luminous life of Christ. As His followers it must always be our method to seek our answers by looking at His life.

There is one passage which immediately comes to mind, John 6. Jesus has just fed the five thousand. He walks halfway back to Capernaum *on the water!* The crowds have begun to follow Him in droves. He is becoming a celebrity. Fame and fortune are His. A record deal looms on the horizon. The disciples are congratulating themselves—they have hitched their wagon to a star. Hats and T-shirts are already being printed up.

In the midst of the adulation, as He is swimming in approval, Jesus begins to talk about the "bread of heaven." This bread, He says, is in fact His flesh which He will give for the life of the world.

Understandably, the kosher crowd begins to grumble. It is at this precise moment that things could go in either of two directions. Jesus could stop and explain the image, calm the people, regain His place in the polls. Or He can do exactly what He proceeds to do.

"No, my flesh is real food and my blood is real drink," He says to the horror of His soon to be ex-followers.

Not only does the crowd leave in disgust, John tells us that many of Jesus' disciples turned back and no longer followed Him. When things might have gone so successfully and so well, He 'blows it,' as, in fact, He will do on every other such occasion.

The meaning of Jesus' words concerning His flesh and blood is not what we are interested in here. This is one of the mysteries of the Faith. What concerns us is the fact that given the choice, Jesus chooses to disregard fame and celebrity-ism. "If I glorify myself, my glory means nothing," He says in John 8:54. And this is just as true for us as for Jesus.

Paul tells us that Jesus had the kind of value system that "did not consider equality with God a thing to be grasped" (Phil. 2:6). The constant posture of Jesus in not that of celebrity but of servant, a footwasher (John 13), a maker of breakfast (John 21). The life of Jesus makes the answer to our original question clear: fame, glory, celebrity have nothing to do with those who follow Christ. His command condemns the seeking of it (Matt. 23:12; Luke 14:7ff).

Don't misunderstand, fame may come for any number of reasons: beauty, talent, circumstance. In our industry it is usually bought. But the follower of Jesus must always choose faithfulness over fame. Given the choice, we must wash feet, not do encores.

The true purpose of Christian music, which many have still not forgotten, is to spread the fame of Jesus Christ, to make Him a celebrity by celebrating Him. This is in fact the only unique, defining characteristic feature of Christian music. It points to Christ. Stylistically there is nothing that sets it apart. Christian music can adopt any number of styles. This is purposeful as we seek to reach out in every possible musical language. There is no longer anything distinctive about our production values. They now equal the level of any other form of music.

The single difference between mainstream and Christian music is the call and privilege of pointing away from ourselves and only to Christ. To deny this privilege and point to the artist is to melt into the drab glitter of the American music culture, to blend in with artists who have nothing higher or greater to point to than themselves. And this is precisely the precipice upon which Christian music is poised. The answer is not in the faceless, heartless, industry of Christian music, but in the warm, forgiving, and encouraging face of Jesus. We must learn, and soon, to stop expecting anything other than the industrial from the industry. The hope lies in the hearts of men and women, artists and business people who comprise what used to be the community of Christian music.

The choice is clear after all and not the dilemma we would have it to be. "Choose this day who you will serve," the Bible says.

In his wonderful new book, *Windows of the Soul*, Ken Gire tells a story of Gustave Dore, the famous artist. Once one of his students presented him with a portrait of Jesus, seeking Dore's artistic critique. He looked at the picture for a long time, searching for the right words. Finally, he handed it back to the student. His critique of the portrait might well be a critique of Christian music as well. Dore told the young artist, "If you loved Him more, you would have painted Him better."

We don't need more money or worldly connections, we need to "love Him more."

Independence Vs. Codependence

John J. Thompson

John Thompson is the founder of True Tunes Etcetera, a leading Christian music store. In 1990 he established a mail order service advertising bestselling and hard-to-find Christian music in his True Tunes News *magazine. He wrote two books in 1994 for David C. Cook Publishers:* Sound Expressions *and* Sound Alternatives, *both designed to introduce young people, parents, and youth leaders to modern Christian music.*

"Be ye not unequally yoked together with unbelievers . . ."
(2 Corinthians 6:14 KJV)

Of course, the contextual meaning of this text refers to marriage between Christians and non-Christians, but, as with many truths in the Word, it can be applied in many ways. The word-picture is that of two oxen hooked to one yoke, one being of greater strength than the other. The weight of the yoke is unevenly distributed. The stronger ox is better off by itself.

This image can apply to issues of vision as well. Too many artists find themselves unequally yoked with record companies that don't share their vision. They're made to pull a disproportionate amount of weight and, yes, they may well be better off by themselves.

THE MUSIC INDUSTRY: LOVE IT OR . . .

Since the '50s, young artists have been spoon-fed the rock and roll dream. Start a band, record a demo, play some big gigs, and get discovered. From there they expect to record breathtaking albums in lush studios and to be paid nicely for their services. Add the fervor of a freshly awakened faith to the formula and you come up with a package deal that promises to satisfy the individual's artistic and spiritual yearnings. Perhaps it's an unconscious expectation, but we all know it's there.

So many of us are predisposed to unequal and even co-dependent relationships with "the industry." An individual may have a specific vision of where to go with his or her craft, but as soon as the label's desired direction differs from that of the artist, the artist assumes the compromise is part of the deal. Often the compromise won't even be presented until the artist is well along the road. With few exceptions, it will happen.

I started a band with my best friend when I was fourteen, recorded demo after demo, and got local opening slots with some of the best touring bands in the industry. Then we negotiated with some labels and got a deal. We released a CD that represented, to us, more than seven years of our lives. To several of the involved business people, we represented cash flow, and possibly nothing else.

I was crushed. Our little record was far from perfect, but it generated good radio airplay, positive reviews, and some great playing opportunities. Additionally, a song composed by my wife about the grief that follows an abortion was used by several pro-life groups as a sort of anthem. Despite all that, an associate at the distribution label decided that eight months was long enough for the record to be "pushed", and he discontinued it. The vision we had for that project wasn't shared by some of the label executives on the business level. But the hardest part to deal with was the realization that it really wasn't their job to share the vision.

So the question is, whose job is it? Who is the keeper of the flame? How can we protect the inspiration while enduring the perspiration?

Independence Vs. Codependence

There are myriad means of safeguarding our passion, including the original impulse (hopefully divine) that started us down this path. Among these means, what I specifically want to address is the issue of independence versus co-dependence. At the risk of sounding like a radio psychologist, I believe the term "co-dependent" is appropriate in this discussion. If you disagree, please read: "record deal."

BRASS TACKS

A contract between an artist and a record company is sort of like a marriage; each party brings something to the relationship. The artist brings a gift and, hopefully, some well-honed talent, as well as his or her unique inspiration and vision. The record company offers distribution, publicity, copyrighting, opportunity, and—of course—cash. Two distinctly different packages, each dependent upon the other to prosper. The artist needs the label to help turn his dream into a career, and the record executive will hit the unemployment line faster than an anorexic pig without the artist's work to sell. But is it an even trade? Is there an alternative?

History shows that if a relationship in this context is not profitable, and one party or the other is to go home empty-handed, it won't be the company. Record companies are businesses. It's not immoral for them to strive for profitability. But too often the biggest mistake an artist makes is not under-

John J. Thompson

standing and accepting that he's there to help the mother ship make payroll. Too often the artist is actually convinced that the company exists to help him further his art.

Although there are a few stories floating around about labels that really put the artists' needs above their own, these labels are rare indeed. Even the most well-intentioned companies must cover their expenses in order to stay in business. You might want to believe that your A & R person is more into your tape than anything else he's ever heard, and that may be true. But at some point that A & R guy has to turn over the master tapes to the marketing department and the radio folks. Then the process begins. The artist may not see his project again until it's on store shelves. It's what happens during the process that can bewilder unwary musicians.

It is crucial that all parties know exactly what they're getting into. Even if you really believe in the people who are courting you, this is what lawyers are for. If a company has nothing to hide, it will not be fearful if you involve a lawyer throughout the contract process. If the company balks at the idea, walk away. It's obviously looking for someone who will let it have its way. If the lawyer believes your interests are being well- served, and your pastor (and parents, if you are still of that age) agree, then you're ready to consider one last thing: Why do you want a record deal to begin with?

Most people assume they cannot have a legitimate musical career or music ministry without a label's logo on their project. This assumption is entirely untrue. Now, especially with the continually lowering prices of high-tech, low-budget studios, as well as desktop publishing, it's almost easy for someone to record an entire album, of considerable quality, for just a few thousand dollars. The big-time budgets of $100,000 and up (all of which is recouped before the artist sees a dime) are no longer necessary. Sure, it's fun to sit in a posh studio eating catered meals and seeing your face in magazine ads and music videos, but remember: you're paying for all that.

It is indeed rare for a debut album on a major label to recoup its costs and actually start generating royalties for the artist. However, if you spend even as much as $5,000 on an indy, and sell each CD for just $10, you need only sell 500 copies to recoup your budget. Plus, you still own your publishing rights (an additional source of revenue, which is almost always gobbled by labels before a writer even knows what they are). You will also not have anyone telling you to change this or alter that so that the product will be more marketable.

In my various experiences I've found that a label release selling 30,000 copies, an independent release that's distributed at wholesale to some retailers selling 5,000 copies, or a direct sale release selling just 1,000 copies will generate the same amount of "profit." Often, a label release will not fully recoup its costs until it has sold more than 150,000 or 200,000 copies. In that case, an artist will make far more money selling 100 copies of an indy than if he sells 50,000 copies through a label. If you play concerts on a regular basis, and if you have any sort of fan base, how difficult can that be?

Now, all this talk of money and sales may have distracted you from my original point. I include these few examples so you can start looking at this from another angle—the bottom line. Remember, it's usually the job of the artist to create, and the company to sell. When an artist doesn't familiarize himself with the "sell" part, he can never be fully assured that he's doing well. You may want to keep your head out of the numbers so that you can focus more clearly on your art or ministry, but I believe that for an artist to entirely leave such things up to someone else, without being actively involved in holding those people accountable, is bad stewardship of the gifts and talents God has given him.

If you don't fully understand the economics of your record deal, you'll never know whether or not you're unequally yoked with a label. Sure, ignorance is bliss when all is well. But when the checks come, or don't come, and you find yourself on the short end of the stick, it will take everything you have in you to keep yourself from becoming jaded and bitter. You don't even want to know what kind of effect those feelings of betrayal and disappointment will have on your art and ministry.

I highly recommend that any individual or band who desires a record deal and a long-term musical career first release at least one independent project. The process of recording, mastering, manufacturing, and marketing your own release will be an invaluable education. If the costs you incur are troubling you, consider those costs as tuition. Besides, if you're good enough to get a deal, you're good enough to recoup on an indy. If you're not quite there yet, at least your name isn't on a contract that renders your life the property of someone else for the next five years.

The process of putting together your own release may also help you hear that still small voice. If you're concerned about God's will for you in this area, then for heaven's sake don't block out your ability to "move when the Spirit says move" by agreeing to follow the instructions of a label exec. If the deal is right, and if God grants you that peace, then you can be assured that He will not lead you astray. But if you've never let Him speak into your life in this way, you'll never know what His voice sounds like.

THE ROAD AHEAD

In closing, I've seen far too many young artists be chewed up and spit out by a machine called The Music Industry (insert the word Christian between "the" and "music" if that's the camp you fall into). In almost every case the disappointment resulted from the artist having been duped. I've also seen artists who've released several major-label projects return to the underground in order to make a living.

I fully believe in the validity of music as a tool for expression, inspiration, and education, and I'm encouraged by the rising presence of Christian music in the mainstream landscape. But I'll be even more excited to see artists and labels working together in mutually beneficial ways. The labels often want to make a difference for God, and so do the artists. But they can become so wrapped up in their own private wrestling match that they're never able to effectively engage the battle. If they can, and we can add to their number countless artists who produce records independently, we'll become a force with which to be reckoned. Then, even when (not if) the affections of the mainstream industry wane, we'll not be rendered useless. Then we'll have the infrastructure necessary to support the artists among us, even when the going gets rough again. And believe me, it will get rough again.

The Practical Side of Independents

How to Make Music, Sell It, and Still Sleep at Night

Michael Hakanson-Stacy

Singer-songwriter Michael Hackanson-Stacy started his own label, Time & Strike Music, in 1992. He has released nine projects—his own recordings, and several acclaimed collections of the traditional blues singer Rev. Dan Smith. His most recent release is Motherless Children: A Collection of Bottleneck Gospel Blues, *a collaborative project whose proceeds will benefit a homeless shelter in Chicago. Michael performs rootsy country gospel blues. His work has been reviewed in almost every major blues publication in the United States. He lives in Springfield, Massachusetts, with his very supportive wife and two daughters.*

People have many reasons why they start a record company or release their own music. Often no existing company is interested in their project. Others turn to putting out their own CDs and cassettes because of their frustration dealing with labels. When I'm asked why I started Time & Strike Music, I usually give the over-simplified answer that I like to sleep soundly at night. Let me explain further.

In addition to performing over the last twenty-plus years, I've worked other jobs in the music business, familiarizing myself with different aspects of the industry. I've worked in retail and wholesale, and I've done promotional work as well. My experiences have been within both the secular and Christian markets. I'd like to share a few things I've observed over the years I've kicked around the business: art gets sacrificed on the altar of greed; morals too often get compromised; and consumers pay a very high price for the finished product.

Since starting my little label in 1992, I've never considered or approached any release on the basis of its commercial viability—whether it would sell a certain number of units. If I feel it is worthy of release, I commit to the project. I've never paid anyone to sell or market a release; to do so is very expensive and the cost is ultimately passed on to the consumer by higher prices. I believe that if the music is art and not just trendy fluff, it will stand up over time and will pretty much sell itself. Unfortunately, most labels give a release very little time to succeed and as a result most releases fail. Longevity is not the trend with most labels.

Michael Hakanson-Stacy

The majority of companies are motivated by money. Too often I have seen projects sold to labels for personal gain (not the artist's) rather than for their worth as art. I've seen people bought off, I've witnessed charts manipulated—it goes on and on; the music gets lost as well as the musician.

Today's consumer is charged a premium for the music they buy on compact disc. Why do CDs cost so much? It costs less to manufacture a CD than it used to cost to press a vinyl record. The wonders of digital technology have lowered production costs even within the last year. So why the high prices? Record company greed, plain and simple. Believe me, most artists are not making a lot of money on royalties and they have to pay a high price for the product they sell at gigs. Rarely do the contracts work in the interest of the artist making the music. It is because of my strong feelings about this that I felt the need to start a label.

So what's involved in putting out your own CD and, perhaps, starting a label? First, you have to record your project—whether on your own recording equipment, or in a studio. If you're going the studio route, plan carefully—pick a studio to fit your needs and your budget. Some studios cater to different types of music and it is important to have a studio and an engineer who have experience with your type of music. Do not be lured into a studio because of its famous name or the supposed "hits" recorded there. This is vanity and you'll be proceeding for the wrong reasons. Get advice from other sensible musicians. Do your homework or you'll be wasting time and money—two valuable resources.

Regarding the manufacture of the CDs themselves, careful shopping is a must. I've seen a 300% variance in replication costs! If you go with a company who does the art work, and the printing of booklets and tray cards, you will pay a much higher rate—and you will lose some control of the project. I would recommend finding a local graphic artist who has a feel for what you're trying to express with the music. I also suggest shopping for a printer yourself, as you can save a lot of money doing the printing separately. Don't leave it to the CD plants—you'll pay one way or the other. When you are ready to deliver the components to the CD plant, remember the method of payment varies; some require different percentages up front. Some will even let you pay with a credit card.

When all the components—your final studio master (on DAT, analog two-track, or CD) or 1630 master (if you have mastering done separate from manufacturing), booklets and traycards, and deposit are in the hands of the pressing plant, they will give you a date when you can expect the finished product (be aware: some are very inaccurate, others are much better with their production timeline). While waiting for the discs we send postcards to our mail-order customers, retailers, and wholesalers announcing the availability of the project. Orders start coming in just as the release arrives.

The temptation will be to send radio DJ copies to all the stations you can. I would advise against it. You'll spend a lot in postage and will be giving away product with little inkling if your music will be played. If you spend money on a cassette-only release, rest assured you won't get airplay! Check with other musicians to find out what radio stations and publications are open to music in your genre. If you don't perform regularly you'll have a tougher time selling your music at the onset. My advice is to start very small and build by word of mouth and, above all, be realistic in your expectations or you will be very disappointed . . . and don't think God is going to do the grassroots work; that's your job.

Many people think it is glamorous to consider themselves full-time musicians and recording artists—that road is long and hard. It will likely put you and your family in a very difficult financial position, and it is not often the responsible avenue to take. I'm a firm believer in tent-making, i.e., working another job. Hey, Paul the apostle sewed a number of seams in his day! Working another job provides for you and your family's physical needs and allows you to put music money back into the business. This way the music can grow much faster. I can't emphasize this enough. If your music evolves into a full-time career in business (and I mean one that will responsibly provide for your needs) then give up your tent-making. However, be sure to count the cost and remember, a well paid full-time music career is the exception and not the rule.

A "do-it-yourself" release of a CD entails a lot of work, but let me assure you the freedom it provides can be very liberating. Just ask anyone who has signed to a label and has experienced trouble getting projects released in a timely fashion. Or worse yet, has been "raked over the coals" trying to get released from a contract with a label which has not been acting in the artist's best interests. I was once signed to a small label. At the outset I was very excited that someone else was going to take care of those seemingly insurmountable costs associated with putting out a record. In the end I was beyond frustration with broken promises and never-ending excuses from the company. In the end, it wasn't worth it . . . so I decided to do it myself and, several releases later, I have never regretted my decision.

I wake up every morning knowing that Time & Strike Music is still around. No one is going to delete my releases because they don't meet some salesperson's expectations. I don't worry about getting cut by the label. Neither do I need to worry about whether the company is honest and based on integrity. No one is going to sell me down the river for a quick buck or a bowl of porridge—or the latest musical trend, for that matter.

I'm at peace knowing I'm personally responsible, and held accountable for my music and my little label. Thanks be to God!

Michael Hakanson-Stacy

Finding the Balance

An Interview with Glenn Kaiser

In many parts of New Zealand "rock music" (i.e., drums and electric instruments) has become so established in church that questions are no longer raised about the appropriateness of the rock medium to church praise and worship. Do you see problems in using rock music in worship?

Excellent question. The word "appropriate" is always a great place to start when choosing musical styles. A very loud band doing full-on rock, even though the lyrics are quite worship oriented, would certainly be out of place in a "typical" communion service in a culturally/spiritually conservative church—especially if most of the congregants are over fifty years old! On the other hand, very mellow (or classical) hymns using King James–era English wouldn't be appropriate for a youth group all-night rave on the beach!—nor for evangelistic outreach to younger listeners in most places.

Previously published in *Reality*. For more information on *Reality* contact the editors at *Reality,* P.O. Box 1562, Paraparaumu Beach 6450, New Zealand.

Asking ourselves if a music style or particular lyrical approach, dress, etc., is appropriate to the situation, audience, or congregation is simple common sense. It is also "loving your neighbor as yourself." It respects the listeners' needs as well as what I would call their "cultural language." Artists who don't are obviously immature, or certainly self-centered in terms of their art.

Of course, much depends on who it is you're communicating with, and what you wish to get across to that particular group. Music appreciation classes have value, but usually Christians—whether younger or older in years—don't relish such education being thrust upon them in church.

Christian musicians tend to put American Christian music on a pedestal: one of our commonest big dreams is to "make it big" in the States. As a consequence we buy into an internationalized, generalized milieu, rather than envisioning how New Zealand Christian artists may be called to speak to our own island nation. Can you comment on how God calls each of us to contextualize the gospel to our own culture, rather than abandoning it in order to hit the big time overseas.

When a musician thinks in terms of mission, the context of how he/she thinks changes. Resurrection Band, or my own solo efforts, are specifically missionary in scope. I happen to be able to speak in several musical languages, or at least dialects, and have found it very helpful to do so as the Lord puts us/me in front of different sorts of people.

Glenn Kaiser

Both here in Chicago (where blues rarely fails to relate) and elsewhere, relating to a crowd is what gives you the right to speak to them. This is true both spiritually and artistically. The sad fact is that not all musicians think in terms of communication and the relative effectiveness of one style or approach over another. As for making it? I can tell you as many horror stories about how Nashville and the CCM industry has trashed lives, marriages, and families as I can recount wonderful stories of redemption and God's blessing on the obedient. My personal definition of making it or success is when artists obey absolutely the confirmed call of God on their lives at all costs.

Certainly there are unique aspects to your culture which must be respected and appreciated, for example, the cultural languages of Maori and pakeha. I question whether Nashville speaks either.

Though I personally have a deep love for New Zealand and visit you as a missionary from time to time, I will repeat what I have said for years: *you* are best suited to lay your life down for your country and people. Don't shuffle off on foreign missionaries the work God has called you to do. As much as we love you, we can't *be* you without the call to actually move there and become truly "Kiwi."

But God help you if as a musician you actually believe that American Christian music—because it is popular—holds some sort of blessing or anointing. I am an American, and very thankful for what God has given us in this country. But

I am also disgusted at how so often we seem to be in the position of dictating spiritual and other policy to the rest of the world. Hear this well: power, money, and popularity do not equal spiritual, artistic, or practical value, and the sooner you learn that the better for everyone.

I suggest that as a nation, you know a lot about sheep! Be careful who you follow. Take from other countries what truly fits, but take care not to import our rubbish—even though it sells.

The Christian public seems to want rock stars—idols, heroes—as much as the secular public does. Is this good—and who ought they to be? Does star status just happen, or is it whipped up by marketing efforts? Do Christian celebrity musicians deserve the special treatment they receive?

Music idols, eh? Try role models and you're talking perhaps Mother Teresa, Billy Graham, or Chuck Colson. Or humble and relative unknowns like your pastor or a godly mum or dad or older church parishioner who never wrote a book, sang a Christian hit song, or appeared on national television. Sure, it's cool to be cool, but the Nash-Vegas cool mill churns them out, then throws them out as soon as unit sales drop off. That's historical fact.

So when we talk heroes, I hope we know better than to think that musical ability mixed with smoke and mirrors has anything to do with godliness. Fiction has its place, but don't confuse it with reality! Forget the mystique, it won't hold a candle to character on Judgment Day.

Glenn Kaiser

Many become musicians because they want people to like them. If they're sufficiently reflective, they realize some time later that being faithful to God and widely liked are not often compatible. What does it mean to seek to serve God and human beings as a Christian musician?

How dare you use the words "musician" and "servant" in the same breath (just kidding)! Even a quick read of the Old Testament (which contains the lion's share of verses relating specifically to music and musicians in Scripture) reveals the following:

Musicians who truly love God are first of all servants. They are of course worshipers and artists, but clearly servants first of all.

You're completely right, many musicians use their musical ability as the centerpiece item in their identity. They use musical skill as currency to purchase admiration, affection, and a sense of self-worth. God save us from the desperately insecure who focus on our approval rather than God's! I can't decide whether they or their adoring/fickle public are the worse for it.

I certainly used music as a personal calling card in the years before I surrendered myself (and it) to Jesus. But I am more and more aware of God's heart and true love for me, so music has become steadily less important. Interestingly, my enjoyment of writing, performing, and recording—as well as opportunities for all three—have only increased. But I enjoy Jesus and people far more than sound waves. Think on that for a moment.

Finding the Balance

You are totally right that being both widely liked and faithful to God is at times incompatible. Do a study on what God says about your words in His book. Then take a good search through Scripture on what He has to say about music (apart from its lyrics). It is very clear that one is far more important to Him than the other.

When you ask, "What does it mean to seek to serve God and human beings as a Christian musician?" I can only answer that many of the practical specifics are relative to what God has confirmed to the individual they ought to be doing.

What is their calling? Do they have adequate biblical, pastoral, and circumstantial direction from God to do what they are doing? Have they really prayed, fasted, sought God and the wise counsel of godly Christians who know them (as well as God's Word) for confirmation? This would be my recipe for anyone, whether we're discussing skills like music, other callings, spiritual gifts, or whether or not to move to Tauranga.

To answer your question generally I would mention things like biblical faith, surrender, and discipleship which all play a part in genuine love for God and others. Local church accountability. Obedience and love for God's Word (Truth!) and issues such as holiness, a consistent biblical lifestyle and witness. On top of this, the willingness to work very hard and yet live a life of (humanly speaking) obscurity. Humility, service, thankfulness.

There is only one rule for all believers, musically challenged or otherwise: "The Lord your God, the Lord is one, and you must love the Lord your God with all of your heart, all of your mind, all of your soul, and all of your strength. You must love your neighbor as yourself."

Don't limit God to this or that dream for your musical ministry, career or whatever it is you'd care to call it. "Give yourselves to humble tasks" (or "associate with the lowly"—take your pick) (Rom.12:16). What about learning or creating tunes for children's church, old folks' homes, hospitals, prisons, parks? Offer your life and music in such situations. Who gives a rip if you're invited to the Grammys? Our sights ought to be set far above that!

How on earth do you think you can do better than doing all you know to do in fulfilling the revealed will of God for your life! Whether the Grammys or the church basement in Rotorua, what's that to you? Christians—therefore Christian musicians—no longer belong to themselves: they are bought at a price.

Jesus says "From those to whom much more is given, much more is required." Remember that those who have international acclaim will one day answer to God for what they did with it. Can anyone debate that some have been excellent witnesses for the Lord while others have been lousy examples of what—by any biblical standard—it means to be a Christian?

Some Christian musicians seek a mainstream audience, while others perform only in church settings. The first group is accused of being worldly, while the second is accused of hiding away in a Christian ghetto. Can you comment on these polarities?

I don't deny that such places as Christian ghettos exist—in fact, American Christians will probably figure a way to franchise them, too. But I suggest a phrase such as "cultural comfort zone" would be closer to the truth. It's safety, familiarity, and comfort we want, wish to assure ourselves of, and guard. Those taking such a stance have little to offer the world in terms of substance and relevance. And in the end this may be for the best.

Some think the devil keeps our art and message hidden in such places. But I think God is doing everyone a service by keeping our foolish or even blemished sacrifices from the hard scrutiny of a secular world! I'm not convinced that God has rejoiced in every offering I've ever brought Him. Let's thank Him for the mercy He shows us (and those who don't yet know Him, when He has either buried or allowed certain products of our ghetto to remain there! Most Christians realize that simply because a thing gets "known" by a large number of unbelievers doesn't mean it will automatically produce positive fruit for the kingdom of God.

God's will is sovereign, whether He takes me to the mainstream music world or not. If He isn't opening the door, I'm not moving in.

Many musicians consider themselves and their offerings very special indeed. Ego does magnify itself, does it not? As we mature, we hopefully have a more accurate picture of our strengths and weaknesses. Accountability—seeking counsel and honest advice from those more experienced and committed to

Jesus than we are—can really help us in this regard.

Another truth I've learned is that being a church musician isn't innately holy. For every proud and self-centered Christian musician in the mainstream scene, there is at least one in every choir.

If you have occasion to hear the many things God is doing among His musician servants (in and out of CCM), I think Christians have less and less to be artistically ashamed of. We should also note that not all pop music lyrics nor artists' lives are patently immoral and base. Yet there is little biblical spirituality offered there.

Some Christian artists have successfully "crossed over" from singing overtly Christian music to making a mark in the mainstream secular market, still as Christians, with less overtly Christian lyrics. But my opinion is that too few Christian musicians are living the sort of Christ-centered, biblically disciplined lives necessary to survive such a trip. I wonder how much of the Cross is actually taken over.

What would you say to young Christians who seem totally absorbed in their music?

Music in itself, art form or career, is equally inept as saviour or lord. So when you find a (typically) young person lusting for the highs the audio drug seems to offer, you are noticing an immature, perhaps deceived, perhaps mistaken person who is still learning. Hey, some of you reading these words were young once! Be gracious. You are surely aware that some of our older brothers and sisters have simply traded the music idol for other idols more in vogue with their current peer group or local congregation.

Musicians need not be one-dimensional people who eat, sleep, and breathe little else but music. But many feel they have nothing else to offer.

A personal relationship with Jesus Christ, coupled with long-term, committed relationships in (if He wills) marriage and family, and participation in a strong Bible-teaching local church, are the stuff of life. Jobs, hobbies, art, all pale in comparison.

If God intended all musicians to do only one specific thing with their music, don't you think something along that narrow line would have been stated somewhere in the Bible? It's amazing how loudly the ignorant rant, particularly about music and God's will for it and for musicians. "Study to show yourself approved." Encourage the believing musicians you know to do likewise. Begin with God's Word!

Let the church (local and large) pray for, teach and give thanks for its musical sons and daughters—just as it must for those who serve in other ways. May the Church do a better and more thorough job of discipling its communicators, and may more musicians truly surrender their dreams and desires to the one who gave them the ability they have in the first place.

May the attitudes and ethics of more and more Christian musicians truly reflect love for Jesus, genuine humility, and respect for the rest of the church—whether their (my) music

Glenn Kaiser

is accepted or not! May more and more musicians come to realize God's love for the Church—imperfect as she is—and may we link tightly in the grace and Lordship of Jesus Christ.

Music in God's Purposes

Jeremy Begbie

Jeremy Begbie is vice principal at Ridley Hall, Cambridge, a theological college training men and women for ordained ministry in the Church of England. There and at Cambridge University he teaches systematic theology. He studied philosophy and music at Edinburgh University, theology at the University of Aberdeen, and served for three years as a minister in a parish. He is a pianist, oboist, and conductor. He is author of Voicing Creation's Praise: Towards a Theology of the Arts *(T & T Clark, 1991) and is shortly to publish* The Sound of God: Resonances between Theology and Music *(Cambridge University Press).*

Reprinted with permission of The Handsel Press and Jeremy Begbie, from *Music in God's Purposes,* © 1989 by Jeremy Begbie. Published by The Handsel Press Ltd.

Music of all sorts has always fascinated and captivated me, and until about eleven years ago, I was set firmly on course to pursue a career as a musician. Even after I followed a call to ordination, my enthusiasm for music remained undiminished. But I soon discovered that remarkably little had been written about the relationship between the gospel and music, about how the central truths of the Christian faith might relate to the world of Beethoven, Mahler, Stravinsky, the Eurhythmics, and U2. Urged on by musicians and theologians much better equipped than myself, I have attempted to help fill that gap by sketching the outline of a Christian perspective on music.

Two comments need to be made at the outset. First, what Christian thinking there is in this area tends to focus exclusively on music in the context of worship. Important as this field is, I believe that too little time nowadays is given to thinking about what God might be saying to us through so-called secular music and how we might better support Christian musicians who make their living amongst people who do not find the church either a problem or an interest. I have therefore deliberately avoided making music in worship a central topic in the hope that if we keep our sights as wide as possible we will gain a much better understanding of the place of music in God's world.

Second, Christian discussions about music which do look beyond the walls of the church all too quickly gravitate around ethical questions: Should the Christian be involved with the pop culture? How are we to react to works like Verdi's *Requiem,* written by a man who disclaimed any faith? Should we allow Christian rock bands in worship when so many rock musicians have been involved with the drug world? Of course these are legitimate concerns, but I doubt if they can be tackled properly unless we set them against a broader canvas. Thus in what follows I have tried to shift the center of the discussion from ethics to theology, from questions about what is "acceptable" or "unacceptable" to questions about how music might fit into God's overall purposes for creation as a whole.

I am all too aware of what I have not had space to consider in any depth—for example: the whole field of non-Western music. I have left many questions unanswered and a number of arguments open-ended. But I have tried to highlight what I believe to be the most fruitful lines of inquiry for those who are keen to link music with a Christian vision of reality. My strongest hope is that, if you will forgive what might be seen as a musical metaphor, I shall stimulate others to take up the baton.

The substance of this chapter was given as a talk to a gathering of undergraduates in Cambridge, and I have tried to preserve something of the character of an address. I am thankful to Don Humphries and Mary Hayter and the students of the Holy Trinity Pastorate for the opportunity to share these ideas with them and for their lively response. I am also extremely grateful to many others—musical and nonmusical—who have helped me with their wisdom and encouragement, in particular Hugo de Waal, Andrew Watson, and most of all, my wife Rachel.

OVERTURE

Music—an Important Issue?

I expect there are many who would think that giving any serious thought to this topic is a colossal waste of time. Most Christians would admit that music ought to be brought under the Lordship of Christ—no less than any aspect of culture, it stands under the promise and judgment of God. Yet, in comparison with the monumental dilemmas of our age— the ecological crisis, population explosion, mass starvation— music seems dwarfed in significance. After all, some would say, music is really only a distraction from the serious problems of life, an entertainment, an amusing luxury for those who have time to enjoy it. Why spend time on this subject when there are so many more important concerns claiming the Christian's attention?

Why indeed? I would offer the following reasons. First, *we are surrounded by music.* The increasing availability of music means that hardly a day passes when we hear none at all, whether Palestrina or nostalgia, Cherubini or hard rock, funk or Verdi. For a modest price we can listen to the world's great orchestras and bands without even leaving our living rooms.

The radio channels provide us with virtually nonstop music to suit every taste. Moreover, music will bombard us whether we choose to listen to it or not: in the dentist's waiting room, the hairdresser's, in boutiques, restaurants, shopping centers, airports, and factories. Would it not be strange, to say the least, if there were no distinctively Christian comment to make on so omnipresent a feature of our culture?

Second, *music holds a place of importance* in most people's lives. The majority of the population spends considerable amounts of time (and money) listening to music of one sort or another. It cannot be glibly dismissed as an adjunct of gracious living. To see music as a disposable luxury for the lucky few flies in the face of the evidence. In 1987, the British public was prepared to pay a total of $1.5 billion on singles, LPs, cassettes and compact discs, and there is little to suggest that the tide is turning, for this figure represents an increase of 23.2 percent on 1986. Very few homes in the country lack music-playing equipment of some description. Successive British governments also seem to believe that giving financial support to music is necessary and desirable (although some are more generous than others!). A Christian account of man can hardly afford to ignore an activity in which people are prepared to invest so much of their resources.

Closely related to this last point is a third: music has *enormous psychological power.* Quite *how* music achieves its effect and the extent of its influence are matters of fierce controversy but few doubt that music can call forth the deepest things of the human spirit and affect behavior in a variety of ways. Factory workers appear to be relieved of boredom and fatigue when treated to background music. Warriors seem to forget their fear and rush into battle on hearing the sound of the bagpipes or war drums. The mentally ill have been helped to health through music therapy. It was this potential of music to alter human behavior which so worried Plato as he painted his ideal of political life in *The Republic*. It also lies behind John Calvin's extreme caution over music in worship: he was prepared to permit only the singing of psalms, and that without harmony and with no musical instruments. And it explains why totalitarian regimes are so anxious about music inculcating subversive ideology. Indeed, Russia had severe restrictions on rock music; even jazz—a proletariat invention!—was fiercely suppressed under Stalin. In the face of all this, the Christian will naturally want to ask whether the power of music is being harnessed today as wisely as it might.

Fourth, *most of the music we hear comes from sources which are not explicitly Christian.* This suggests something very serious about the impact of the Church in society. If God's Spirit is active in a unique way among those who proclaim Christ as Lord, then the Church should surely be where the most enriching and exciting art is being produced, or at the very least, be the most vibrant inspirer of the arts in society. But who would seriously claim this today? Christians have hardly been the pioneers of the musical innovations of this century. Indeed, it is difficult to point to a specifically Christian "style" in twentieth-century music. It would be unfair to say that church music is the refuge for all the music unfit for theater or concert hall but there would be more than a grain of truth in the comment. A hard and careful look at where music fits into the Christian scheme of things might give us a clue as to what has gone wrong here, as well as pave the way for a more effective Christian contribution to the music of our age.

Fifth, since the mid-1950s, a kind of music usually classed as *"rock" or "pop" has been a major feature of the musical landscape of the West.* It has generated a heated debate among Christians, resulting in a wide spectrum of opinions ranging from warm-hearted embrace to bitter hostility. A few years ago, the controversy was given a new impetus by John Blanchard's blistering attack on the pop scene and the hazards of using rock music in evangelism.[1] Can the thoughtful Christian opt out of the debate, especially when we bear in mind that rock music is increasingly used in the Church's worship and witness, that there have been a striking number of converts from the pop/rock world in recent years, and that about 80 percent of the British population chooses it as their favorite brand of music?

Sixth, although some may be cynical about the present state of church music, through the ages *music has normally had a key part to play in the worship of the Church.* There have, of course, been periods when it has fallen into neglect, and very occasionally, dismissed altogether. Yet in general, a glance at church history confirms that music has usually been seen as a

1. John Blanchard, *Pop Goes the Gospel* (n.p.: Evangelical Press. 1983).

vital component in worship. Is it not worth asking why this is so, and just how it is that music can glorify God?

"I Know What I Like, and That's All That Matters"

There is another reason why some might think that there is little point in trying to develop a Christian view of music, namely, that all appraisals of music seem to be inescapably subjective, shaped by our own tastes and the influences of our culture. It is hard enough finding consensus in Christian ethics; it is even harder in musical aesthetics. Any conclusions we might come to about what makes a piece "good" or "bad," for example, will be either arbitrary or die the death of a thousand qualifications. Some would go further and say that there are in fact no objective standards, no norms by which music can be interpreted and assessed. Such a position—usually called "relativism"—holds that judgments about value and quality in music are no more than expressions of inherited assumptions of our culture, or of our own individual likes and dislikes. With this often goes a deep-seated assumption in the West that it is science which provides us with undisputed facts and truth, while the arts move in a separate sphere of cultural conditioning or private taste.

I can feel the force of this kind of objection, yet I think it is overstated. The Christian faith presents us with a vision of what is the case about the world whether we choose to appreciate it or not. It speaks of the ultimate purpose of existence, the intention of God for all human beings, the nature of God's relationship to the world, and the final goal of the whole cosmos. And there is every reason to believe that music is quite capable of giving voice to these fundamental truths (and of denying them), even though it may do so in a less direct way than in the sciences. Of course personal preference has a large part to play in the way we respond to music, as do the values of our social group, but to lose our moorings in objective truth altogether and set ourselves adrift in the uncharted seas of "I know what I like and that's all that matters" is intolerable. Developing a Christian perspective on music may be arduous, but to abandon the task in despair is surely not a viable option. (Ironically, most of us do speak about the arts in a way which suggests implicitly, even if not explicitly, that we are working with some kind of objective criteria of value. The debate about government aid to the arts provokes many lengthy speeches about "maintaining standards." In the same way, we may speak of having our own tastes in music, but many of us also talk about "educating" taste, "acquiring" taste and "improving" taste.)

What Is Music?

Having attempted a defense of our subject, we must now ask: just what is music? Whole libraries have been written in response to this question, but at the very least, we need to say three things.

In the first place, music is a form of human engagement with the *physical, created world*. It involves working with the raw material of creation, taking sounds, arranging and combining them into various meaningful patterns of pitch, rhythm, and volume to make a coherent whole. Hence, to approach music theologically will mean looking carefully at the nature of the world brought into being and sustained by God, as well as our place in it.

Secondly, music *communicates human values;* it reflects commitments and convictions about what is true, good, or beautiful. This may seem obvious, but it is not taken for granted by all. Indeed, some have vigorously challenged the idea that music refers to anything beyond itself. Proponents of what is usually called "formalism" insist that the meaning of piece of music is only *in* the music. A symphony, for example, is not "about" the composer's emotions, deepest longings, or whatever. It has no meaning outside itself. So argued the composer Igor Stravinsky, and his line has been taken up with an almost crusading energy by Pierre Boulez, the contemporary French composer and conductor. However, even the most ardent formalists have conceded that all music bears at least some recognizable relationship to the world of human values. Music is humanly organized sound and will inevitably convey certain assumptions and beliefs. In certain cases, of course, it is very hard to pin down these values. Some composers wear their hearts very much on their sleeves, but others are a good deal more obscure: the music of Wagner is much less ambiguous than that of, say,

Ravel. Nevertheless, my main point still holds: all music conveys, to a lesser or greater extent, human values—even, as many have pointed out, the music of Pierre Boulez!

But we must add a third point: *music is not merely a vehicle for conveying a message.* The opposite to the formalists' position is to see music as if it were simply a medium through which a message is channeled, the important thing being the message, not the medium. This too is unacceptable. For in most cases, we cannot separate the meaning of a piece of music from the music itself. What, for instance, is the "message" of Beethoven's Seventh Symphony? It may convey to us a sense of joy, animation, ebullience, or whatever, but in so doing it would be absurd to claim that we have captured its entire meaning. Its meaning can only be appreciated by listening to music. Even when the composer's ideals, worldview, or whatever are clearly displayed in a piece of music, we cannot distill this into a concise statement which can then be set apart from the music, examined and assessed.

It is very important for Christians to grasp this, for often we have fallen prey to the idea that in music we can detach the medium from the message, the form from the content. To take one example, some believe that we can "Christianize" rock music simply by giving it new lyrics. Larry Norman, one of the best-known performers in the Christian pop world, claims that "The sonic structure of music is basically neutral. It's available to anyone to express the kind of message they choose."[2] But the weight of evidence indicates the opposite,

2. As quoted in Blanchard, *Pop Goes the Gospel,* 81.

namely that the sonic structure of music does convey its own meaning. An aesthetically inept song remains inept however scriptural the words might be. The pertinent question to ask of Christian rock music is: what can the gospel do to the music? To take another example, there are those who believe that the only music which can qualify for divine approval is that with a clear gospel message tagged on to it. But this is hopelessly restrictive, for it overlooks the fact that music by itself can be a perfectly valid way of bringing glory to God. We may blame the former Soviet Union for stifling the arts, but some Christians score no better with their insistence that only a kind of evangelical aural propaganda could ever please God. To adapt a phrase of Hans Rookmaaker, "music needs no justification."[3] Or, as Peter Smith, a Christian painter, puts it, "Once the pressure is there to make a painting 'message-oriented' there is a strong tendency to undervalue or ignore the reality of a painting as a painting."[4] Just the same applies to music.

The "Romantic" and the "Puritan"

To set the stage for the main part of our discussion, and to highlight the key issues involved, let me compare two very different attitudes to music, each with a long history and by no means absent today.

3. See Hans Rookmaaker, *Art Needs No Justification* (n.p.: InterVarsity Press, 1978).
4. In Tim Dean and David Porter, eds., *Art in Question* (n.p.: Marshall Morgan and Scott, 1987), 115.

First, there is what we can call the "romantic" attitude: that music by its very nature has the power to grant us some kind of immediate communion with God in a way which mediates healing and forgiveness, that God is in some way to be encountered *in* music. Such an approach reappears many times and in many guises in musical history. It comes to the fore in the nineteenth century, particularly with the German Romantics, and often goes hand in hand with a view of the composer as a sort of high priest or prophet, endowed with an especially acute insight into ultimate truth. Brahms is said to have remarked to Clara Schumann, "While others have religion, we have something better." Listen to C. S. Lewis recalling his childhood love of Wagner:

> To a boy . . . whose highest musical experience had been Sullivan, the *Ride [of the Valkyries]* came like a thunderbolt. From that moment Wagnerian records . . . became the chief drain on my pocket money and the presents I invariably asked for. . . .
>
> Asgard and the Valkyries seemed to me incomparably more important than anything else in my experience. . . . Unless I am greatly mistaken *there was in it something very like adoration, some kind of quite disinterested self-abandonment* to an object which securely claimed this by simply being the object it was.[5]

Wagner would certainly have appreciated Lewis's sentiments. In a similar vein, Anton von Webern (1883–1945), one

5. C. S. Lewis, *Surprised by Joy* (n.p.: Collins, 1955), 64. My italics.

of the foremost composers at the turn of the century, believed that the the music he advocated and composed would draw the listener into an experience of the spiritual force governing and supporting all things—what he called the "World." More recently, Karlheinz Stockhausen, prince of the musical avant-garde, has espoused a similar philosophy. In a different way, some are quite convinced that rock music frequently sets itself up as a substitute religion. The mysterious smoke-filled atmosphere, the steady dull pulse, the priest-performers carrying their electronic ceremonial gear, the gathering of the faithful followers—all this seems to carry religious overtones. Rock musician Tom McSloy has said bluntly: "To *get* into rock you have to *give* in to it, let it inside, flow with it to the point where it consumes you, and all you can feel or hear or think about is the music."[6] Certainly, films such as Prince's *Purple Rain* seem to carry the implication that music can be a vehicle of salvation.

At the opposite end of the spectrum lies the "puritan" attitude.[7] The musical puritan frowns on any form of romanticism. Yes, music has enormous power to move and stir, but just because it is so potent it needs to be handled with extreme care. Only God can save, when his Word is heard and received by repentance and faith in Christ. Music's strong links with the entertainment world should make us doubly cautious

6. *National Review,* 30 June 1970.

7. I am not using the word strictly; I am speaking of a general attitude which only sometimes overlaps with the opinions of the sixteenth- and seventeenth-century Puritans.

about succumbing to its potential hazards. The only music fit for God is that used in Christian worship, composed and performed by Christians. Some go further still and insist that music can only honor God if it is harnessed to an unmistakable Christian message. Such opinions were not uncommon in branches of the evangelical revival of the late eighteenth century, and are still to be met in the more extreme Protestant wings of the church today.

But as I see it, neither of these two positions is plausible: the first because its claims for music are too extravagant; the second because, as I have already argued, music can bring praise to God in its own right, even when it is not accompanied by overtly Christian words. It is now our task to suggest a third way ahead.

MAIN THEMES

Music, I have said, is one of the ways in which we shape and mold what we are given in creation. I propose now to outline the major themes which make up a Christian account of the created world and our role in it, before going on to ask how music relates to these themes.

Order and Contingence

First, we must speak of the order of the world. Every day of our lives, we are sustained by the belief that the world we inhabit is pervaded with order, that the universe is not a chaotic jumble of disconnected and completely random events, but one of coherence and regularity. Without this basic conviction our lives would become virtually impossible. The natural sciences would grind to a halt, for to make any progress at all they have to assume that the world they observe and study is inherently intelligible. The orderliness, the Christian will want to add, speaks powerfully of the wisdom and beauty of the God who brought all things into existence.

At the same time, second, the world cannot account for itself. It is not self-explanatory, but points away from itself to God. As the philosophers would say, it is contingent; as the psalmists would say, it worships God (Pss. 96: 11–12; 98:8–9). The meaning of the world as a whole will only be discovered when we look beyond it to the God who made it, sustains it, and draws it towards its goal. Thus the universe is not some kind of self-contained machine, whose movement through time is simply the unfolding of its own rigid and built-in laws, Indeed, advances in physics during this century have rendered such a view implausible. The picture emerging is more that of an "open" system, a finite universe, exhibiting a subtle interplay between law and circumstance, being and becoming, necessity and chance. Creation is constantly surprising us, showing an astonishing capacity for development and change which gives rise to ever richer patterns of order. For Christians this is immensely important, for they believe that although the world has been given a measure of autonomy by God, it is nevertheless open to his creative activity. If we lose sight of this, we are in danger of lapsing into idolatry—the attempt to make something *within* the world final and ultimate, and to bow down and worship it. As Paul would say, we shall find ourselves worshiping the creature rather than the Creator (Rom. 1:25).

God's Commitment to Creation as a Whole

Closely related to order and contingence is a third theme: God's love of all that He has made, His unremitting faithfulness to the whole of creation, "And God saw everything that He had made, and behold, it was very good." (Gen. 1:31 RSV). It makes no sense to restrict God's love to mankind. For it was all things which God brought into existence out of nothing as an expression of His love, making Himself vulnerable to the rejection which the world's independence might bring. Similarly, it is every atom and molecule of the created order which God upholds out of love, refusing to let it disintegrate. And by coming amongst us as a creature of flesh and blood in Jesus, and through the Resurrection of the body of Jesus, God has shown us that it is the whole of creation which He longs to re-make at the end of history. What God is toward creation will not contradict what He is towards you and me in Jesus Christ. Because God *is* love in His innermost heart, all His acts are acts of love. He is committed to the entire physical and natural order with just that intensity of love which took Jesus to the cross for our sin. Surely this is part of what lies behind those remarkable assertions in the New Testament which speak of Christ as being the one "through whom" all things were created (John 1:10; Col. 1:16; Heb. 1:2). In the life, death, and Resurrection of Christ, we see not only God's saving purposes for mankind, but also for the entire created universe.

Our Calling as Priests of Creation

Our fourth theme concerns our role in the natural world. Where do we fit in this grand cosmic drama? The best way of answering that is to describe ourselves as "priests of creation." The Bible speaks many times of creation praising God; it is our role to extend that worship, to enable creation to glorify its Maker in a way that it could never do if it were left to itself. This has a number of facets to it. It will involve *discovery*. We are to bring what is latent in creation to the surface, to explore its harmony and symmetry, to be perceptive to its hidden glories. There will be *respect* for what we are given in creation. If God is committed in love to His world, and love entails honoring another's integrity, then our own attitude to our natural environment should display the same loving respect. There is also the obligation to *develop* what is given in creation. In Genesis 1:28, God blessed man and woman saying, "Be fruitful and multiply, and fill the earth and subdue it; and have dominion over the fish of the sea and over the birds of the air and over every living thing"(RSV); and in Genesis 2:15, "God took the man and put him in the garden of Eden to till it and keep it"(RSV). Our task is not simply to sit back and enjoy creation, but to take what is potential and make it actual: to harvest the sea, plough the ground, harness the elements, and bring forth new forms of order not immediately given "in the beginning." Further, all of this is to be carried out *with others and for the good of others.* The biblical picture of man and woman makes it clear that we were made not to pursue self-fulfillment in isolation, but to find fulfillment in relationship with others, in loving and being loved, and to be responsible to God for the created world in which we live.

Order out of Disorder

I have spoken of the pervasive order of the world. But surely there is something obvious I have neglected. What about disorder? What about the diseases, earthquakes, tidal waves, floods, and droughts which wreak havoc in creation? And what are we to say about sin, that tragic self-centered bias in our own nature which has destroyed our relationship with God and our dealings with each other? How do we make sense of this in a supposedly ordered world?

This brings us to our fifth theme: order out of disorder. The mystery of evil will never be unraveled in this life, yet the staggering claim of our faith is that God's unceasing love for creation has led Him to come as a man in Jesus, submit on the cross to the forces of destruction and chaos, and through the raising of Jesus from the dead, forge out of the most evil event in history a new and splendid glory. This is the meaning of the divine judgment enacted in Christ: God has not simply destroyed evil, but has placed Himself under its power and disorder so that He can wrest out of it a new order. In Jesus Christ, crucified and risen, we see our humanity renewed. In Him, we also see physical matter transformed. And in Him we have a pledge that one day all things will be made new—as Paul expresses it in Romans 8, set free from bondage to decay. Such is the dazzling future—a new heaven and a new earth—to which even now we are being led.

This of course makes our own role in creation even richer. For the miracle of the gospel is not just that we can be forgiven and can find peace with God, but that out of sheer grace God invites us to share in His mission of renewal to creation, to bring order out of disorder, sense out of senselessness, healing out of sickness, and deliverance out of tragedy.

Through the Spirit of Jesus Christ

A sixth theme needs to be added. We are never more truly "priests of creation" than when we are made one with Christ through the Spirit, when the one true High Priest makes us priests with Him. For it is in Him that creation has been re-ordered towards God, and through Him that as God's people we can be rightly related to the natural world. At the profoundest level, it is only as we are in Christ that we will be able to discern aright the latent order of creation (and not misread its disorder), develop it, and redeem it. Does this not lie behind the second chapter of the Epistle to the Hebrews? For there we read that Christ, the true High Priest (v. 17), for whom and by whom all things exist (v. 10), is the one who stands in our midst, leading us in our worship of the Creator: "I will proclaim thy name to my brethren, in the midst of the congregation I will praise thee" (v. 12 RSV).

COUNTERPOINT

By now, I expect the reader is getting restless. What has all this to do with music? The answer will be found if we now examine music from the point of view of each of the six themes we have just outlined.

I have argued that nature is pervaded with a God-given order. Whatever else we say about music, if it is to honor God the Creator, then to some degree it should reflect and bear witness to this basic order permeating all things.

To make such a claim about any of the arts today is to risk being called old-fashioned and reactionary. Indeed, the notion that music is an engagement with some kind of objective order has not only been questioned but strongly opposed—Boulez, for instance, explicitly repudiates the idea. The burgeoning of electronic music in the last few decades places the emphasis very firmly on manipulating sounds rather than responding to what nature presents to us, bringing a degree of artificiality which music has never had before. Nowadays the underlying assumption is that the artist must bring order to a world which makes very little sense on its own, drawing on the reservoir of inward experience or on a sophisticated system of order he has developed himself. Needless to say, this has resulted in a widespread distrust of the traditional musical conventions and assumptions of the West: rhythms are disintegrated, questions about consonance or dissonance are usually irrelevant, and harmonic movement is very often abandoned completely. Stockhausen, in the preface to his *Kontra-Punkte* (1952–53), explains that in this work there is:

> No repetition, no variation, no development, no contrast. All these presuppose "figures"—themes, motives, objects—which are repeated, varied, developed and contrasted; dissected, manipulated, magnified, reduced, modulated, transposed, mirrored or retro-graded. *All that has been given up. . . . Our world—our language—our grammar.*[8]

Taken to its extreme, this gives rise to a conscious attempt to destroy form and order altogether. A whole genre of music has arisen in which what emerges by chance is seen as more important than anything that can be prepared. Indeterminacy "rules." We are left entirely to the whim of the performer and the circumstances of the performance, and must not attempt to "make sense" of what we hear. John Cage, the most famous exponent of "aleatoric" music, claims of his own work: "Value judgments are not in the nature of this work as regards either

8. Karlheinz Stockhausen, preface to *Kontra-Punkte* (n.p., 1952–53). My italics.

composition performance, or listening". His *Imaginary Landscape No. 4* (1951) is performed by a conductor and twelve radios, with two players at each, one for tuning and the other for dynamics. (The first "performance" took place too late in the evening for there to be much on the radio!) Such "music" is deliberately intended to provoke us into asking whether we and the music we make, and indeed whether all human achievements, are not merely accidental events in a random universe.

There is something attractive about a component of chance interlaced with determinism in music, which might correspond to that interweaving of spontaneity and necessity which seems to lie at the heart of the physical world. (Perhaps jazz, in which improvisation on a given harmonic base is so central, has something vital to teach us here.) But whatever the element of chance in the world, and the disorder that might arise from it, the Christian is committed to the view that order and disorder are not equal opposites, that order is always more predominant and always, as it were, has the last word. That strand of contemporary music which sets out to subvert all order can only strike us as perverse, however much it may betoken the despair and hopelessness of our age.

At this point, I can hear the student of modern music protesting. Setting aside extremists like Cage, there are many works which may seem utterly disordered on first hearing, but which are in fact painstakingly composed according to strictly defined and rigorous principles. Xenakis's elaborate *Terretektorh*

(1965–66) is a case in point, in which logarithmic functions and Archimedean spirals generate a work of intricate mind-stretching complexity. And, so it is often maintained, it always takes time to appreciate and familiarize ourselves with new types of order. After all, what one generation calls chaotic turns out to be engagingly beautiful in another. Nevertheless, the issue is whether highly sophisticated pieces of this type can ever be appreciated by the listener who is not (and perhaps never can be) initiated into the esoteric secrets of their structure. The difficulties we have with such music may be just as great as with works which deliberately defy organization. Composers may revel in a new and intriguing language system, but it will only make sense to the listener if there is at least some shared vocabulary and syntax. Boulez makes a fascinating comment about his *Structures 1a* (1952) when he writes of "an excess of order which is equivalent to disorder."[9] In other words, the important question is not whether order is present but what kind of order it is, and whether it has lost touch with any reality beyond the composer's own inventive mind. On a wider front, the dangers of this tendency to retreat from natural form have been brilliantly charted in Erich Kahler's book *The Disintegration of Form in Arts.*[10]

Our second main theme is also illumination for developing a Christian approach to music. If the world is contingent, pointing beyond itself for an explanation, we need to be wary

9. Quoted in Christopher Butler, *After the Wake: An Essay on the Contemporary Avant-Garde* (n.p.: OUP, 1980), 30 f.
10. Erich Kahler, *The Disintegration of Form in Arts* (n.p.: George Braziller, 1968).

Jeremy Begbie

of the exaggerated and idolatrous claims made about music by the "romantic." Unquestionably, music has the power to soothe, move, stir, and heal, but by itself it is powerless to deal with the root of the human predicament and reconcile us to God. Graham Cray speaks from a wide knowledge of contemporary rock music when he argues:

> The rock scene contains both a genuine power to express alienation in a way that unites the individual with others who experience the same, and an illusion of power that it can change the heart of things. "I just want to be me" is the problem as well as part of the answer, but the whole answer cannot be found through music.[11]

Just as dangerous is treating the musician as somebody blessed with exceptional religious intuition simply by virtue of his calling. The Old Testament prophets saw clearly this pitfall—idolatry often entails not only "worshiping the work of our hand'" but also exalting the craftsman beyond his proper status. Hence Isaiah's stern reminder: "craftsmen are nothing but men" (44:11NIV).

Third, what does God's commitment to creation as a whole say to the musician? It says to him, and indeed to every artist, that he has nothing to be ashamed of just because he is working with the physical realities of sounds. It seriously distorts biblical truth to disparage the material world in the name of some "spiritual" higher reality. Indeed, it is much more helpful and true to the composer's work to see it as a thorough

11. Tom Morton, ed., *Solid Rock* (Pickering & Inglis 1980), 6.

interaction with what we have received at the hand of the Creator rather than as a means of withdrawing into some ethereal world of creative ideas. We would do well to listen to Stravinsky, the foremost composer of our time:

> The very act of putting my work on paper, of, as we say, kneading the dough, is for me inseparable from the pleasure of creation. So far as I am concerned, I cannot separate the spiritual effort from the psychological and physical effort; they confront me on the same level and do not present a hierarchy. The word *artist* which, as it is most generally understood today, bestows on its bearer the highest intellectual prestige, the privilege of being accepted as a pure mind—this pretentious term is in my view entirely incompatible with the role of the *homo faber*.[12]

Fourth, music is one of the many ways in which we fulfill our vocation as priests of creation. In this connection, I spoke of the need to *discover* and *respect* what is given in creation. I have already said quite a bit about music as a witness to the inherent order of creation, but a further aspect of this is worth considering here, namely, the need for the composer to respect his materials. Whether he likes it or not, certain note sequences, combinations of notes, and rhythmic structures have distinctive characteristics which in turn will affect the listener in particular ways, some of them quite predictable.

Here we run into a minefield of argument, for some say that our reaction to music depends entirely on upbringing,

12. Igor Stravinsky, *Poetics of Music in the Form of Six Lessons,* trans. Arthur Knodel and Ingolf Dahl, (n.p., Harvard University Press, 1947), 51.

listening habits, etc., while others insist that music is a universal language rooted deep within the natural order. The truth will probably be found in a combination of both positions. Our culture certainly plays a large part in the way we hear music, as the discipline of ethno-musicology—the study of different sorts of music in their cultural setting—is constantly reminding us. Those who want to dismiss rock music on the grounds that particular kinds of heavy drumming will always induce dangerous physiological effects need to take this point to heart. Research shows that our experience of music turns on much more than physical or acoustical factors alone. On the other hand, it is just as fallacious to assert that music evokes a response in us *solely* on the basis of cultural likes and dislikes. An increasing body of material shows that innate, natural properties of sounds themselves have a key part to play, and that there is a correlation between music and physiological activities such as respiration, cardiovascular patterns, and galvanic skin response. On much the same lines, the American conductor and composer Leonard Bernstein, through an intriguing comparison with the deep and surface structure of language, has argued that at a profound level all music is grounded in a given fact of nature, namely the harmonic series: that set of vibrations which in varying degrees accompanies any note sung or played. "All music," claims Bernstein, "whether folk, pop, symphonic, modal, tonal, atonal, polytonal, microtonal, well-tempered or ill-tempered . . . all of it has a common origin in the universal phenomenon of the harmonic series."[13] He goes on to urge that the attempt to wrestle free from the harmonic series, as evinced in so much twentieth-century music, is in the long run self-defeating. Others have pointed to the existence of universal structural principles in music, such as the use of mirror forms, theme and variation, repetition, etc. It would seem then, even allowing for cultural factors, that the musician cannot simply ignore the natural properties of the components of music nor the physical reactions which they inevitably generate: they will need to be discerned, honored and respected.

Under my fourth theme I also mentioned *development*. A composer not only discovers and respects, he combines sounds in novel ways, he explores fresh melodic lines, he juxtaposes rhythms and harmonies to create new undiscovered meaning. Perhaps this needs to be especially heeded by contemporary rock musicians. Despite the many strengths of pop and rock music (its rhythmic drive, its instant appeal, its social conscience, its ability to speak powerfully to a wide cross section of culture and class), harmonically, with a few notable exceptions, most of the music is remarkably unenterprising and stuck in a mold. Could there be a place here for a more adventurous development of harmony without sacrificing the distinctiveness of the pop idiom?

Needless to say, the development of new musical meaning can make great demands of the listener. Many of us would prefer that music cost us no effort. If we find music hard to

13. Leonard Bernstein, *The Unanswered Question* (n.p., Harvard University Press, 1976), 33.

stomach on first hearing we tend to dismiss it as "nonsense" or "impossible"; if it instantly brings the desired effect, we praise it and perhaps even go out and buy it. Many composers today feel they have little room to experiment, for their prime interest becomes satisfying the consumer as quickly as possible and getting the most lucrative return of their efforts. We ought to thank God that some people thought Beethoven's music worth preserving: much of it was written off at its first performance!

I remember when I first listened to the *War Requiem* by Benjamin Britten. All I could hear was incongruous wailing, disjoined fragments of melody, and turbulent harmonies. It was only on repeated listening that the music began to make an impact on me, and slowly I began to discover its amazing depth. Britten's genius was to a large extent his ability to juxtapose what would normally be unrelated (the *War Requiem* is full of this) and thereby to create remarkably fresh images in sound, but this requires a new type of attentiveness on our part, a widening of our musical vocabulary, an abandoning of some of our long-cherished aural filters. Of course, in some modern music the vocabulary is stretched too far, as I have already suggested, and I am not advocating that we all need to go to evening classes on Britten before we can appreciate *Peter Grimes*. But to romanticize popular culture and allow immediate satisfaction to dictate quality is to risk closing our ears to fresh ways in which creation is being brought to praise its Creator.

The Bible, I have also said, speaks of us finding our fulfill-ment in relationship, in community, not as isolated and self-sufficient individuals. This too has far-reaching consequences for music, for it too is to be practiced *with others and for the good of others.* Very deeply rooted in our imagination is the image of the artist as a lone bohemian, lonely and misunder-stood, eccentric and unconventional. Utterly committed to giving vent to his feelings, he bravely carries on despite his unpopularity. His primary duty is not to his fellow men and women, but to his own inner creative urge. Driven by the passionate search for novelty, he is concerned about his society only insofar as he can make his own unique stamp on it. With this often goes a denigration of the musical past, sometimes leading to a wholesale rejection of all inherited artistic traditions. John Cage outrageously proclaims, "We will cer-tainly listen to this other music—this totally determined music or Beethoven, or whatever, but we'll never again take it seriously."[14]

Of course, by no means does every musician today sees his or her task in this way, but I sense that this cast of mind is still very strong and its influence wide-reaching. We only need think of the confusion which so many feel in the face of much contemporary art, whose inner meaning seems to be accessible only through a secret code available to the privileged few. C. S. Lewis laments:

14. Quoted by Richard Kostelanetz, *John Cage* (n.p., Penguin, 1974), 11.

In the highest aesthetic circles one now hears nothing about the artist's duty to us. It is all about our duty to him. He owes us nothing; we owe him "recognition," even though he has never paid the slightest attention to our tastes, interests, or habits.[15]

This isolation of the artist can be heavily reinforced in a financially competitive society. Paradoxically, commercial pressure on the arts produces not only those who spend energy trying to win popular support, but at the other extreme, those who become obsessed with originality. As Christopher Butler points out, "The art which we recognise as avant-garde may . . . lull us into accepting sheer novelty of experience without, immediately at least, raising questions of value. In a consumer society the serious and the trivial alike profit by being new."[16]

In this connection, a good case can be made for saying that the process of making and enjoying music, by its very nature, has something especially important to teach us about relating to one another. This has recently been argued persuasively by Alexander Goehr in the Reith Lectures. With special reference to the symphony orchestra, he claims

Each participant in the musical process—whether listener, composer or performer—is a principal actor; music has no place for supportive roles. It involves the whole man and demands of him his complete attention. Each individual has

15. C. S. Lewis, *Screwtape Proposes a Toast and Other Pieces* (n.p., Collins,1965), 118.
16. Butler, *After the Wake*, 125 f.

to make music entirely on his own, while remaining in step with everybody else in order that harmony may be achieved. If he is able to speak with his own voice while retaining his proper place, he will indeed be in paradise.

He continues:

Nobody except the most blinkered believer in a core curriculum could again relegate music to an extra-curricular activity, nor deny that among all the arts, it offers a unique model of human relationships. . . . Music is the pursuit of harmony.[17]

It is here that an invigorating dialogue can take place between the Christian and the musician. That a musician should take due account of the expectations of his community is not a sign of failure, it is part and parcel of what it means to love his neighbor, and a recognition that he can only fulfill his task as he relates to others. To quote C. S. Lewis again:

When an artist is in the strict sense working, he of course takes into account the existing tastes, interests and capacity of his audience. These, no less than the language, the marble, the paint, are part of his raw material; to be used, tamed, sublimated, not ignored or defied. Haughty indifference to them is not genius; it is laziness and incompetence.[18]

Similarly, that a composer should know and understand past musical traditions is to acknowledge that his own life is bound up with that of others before him who have shaped his

17. Alexander Goehr, *The Listener,* 31 December 1987, 16.
18. Lewis, *Screwtape Proposes,* 118 f.

Jeremy Begbie

own identity. The attempt to break free from every musical tradition of history is not just impossible to achieve but actually self-destructive, for it destroys even the possibility of learning from the past and impedes effective communication in the present. Indeed, some of the most interesting music of our century has depended on an overt reworking of the traditions of the past, as in Penderecki's *St Luke Passion* (1966), Michael Tippett's *Child of Our Time* (1941), and Peter Maxwell Davies' *Sinfonia* (1968).

I am of course aware that great musical innovators like Beethoven, Wagner, and Stravinsky were often seen by their contemporaries as incomprehensible eccentrics. And no artist is called to a bland conformism out of fear of upsetting the masses. But I am urging that today, we need to be speaking less about self-expression and the inner recesses of a composer's psyche and more about the musician as a communicator, less about escaping from the past and more about drawing on and reshaping our common musical inheritance. I am suggesting that musical imagination and tradition are dependent on each other: imagination, left to itself, runs wild and tradition without imagination stagnates. In Goehr's words, I am hoping that we can encourage artists both to speak with their own voice and retain their proper place. And I am also contending that a Christian account of man's place in the world provides us with just that social perspective which would release so much present-day thinking about the arts from its current malaise.

What bearing does our fifth theme—order out of disorder—have on music? Perhaps it would be best to put it in this way: music which most clearly witnesses to the Christian pattern of creation, fall, and redemption will display the twin elements of *honesty and hope*. By honesty, I mean a sober awareness of evil in all its horror. There must be no attempt to mask or slur over the disorder in the world, or the terrifying history of man's wrongdoing. By hope, I mean an even stronger recognition that, because of what God has accomplished in Jesus, disorder is not the overriding truth about creation, and that sin is not the last word about the human condition.

These elements cannot be held apart. Honesty without hope quickly turns into a paralyzing despair. This is surely the underlying current of a vast amount of twentieth-century art, including some of the music we have mentioned in passing. We cannot afford to be deaf to that message, especially since it is often the arts which provide the most perceptive diagnosis of our true condition. Hans Rookmaaker has written:

> Too many teachers and church leaders do not even try to understand, and do not read books on bomb culture or on the revolt in style. . . . We have not kept abreast of the problems of our age, and have often failed to see how we have lost ground. This was simply because the new unchristian movements were so active in fields in which Christians professed to be ignorant and wanted to remain so, e.g. in theater, art, music and intellectual endeavours.[19]

19. Hans Rookmaker, *The Graduate*, Autumn 1975.

Nevertheless, we must get beyond mere resigned pessimism, and beyond protest for protest's sake. For in Christ, God has grasped evil in all its ugliness and brought out of it a new and living hope. By raising Jesus from death, He has opened up for us a future which will eventually embrace the whole of creation. Any music which dares to bear the name "Christian" will resound with the heartbeat of joy.

By the same token, hope without honesty slides into sentimentalism. To our shame, much so-called "Christian music" has degenerated into a nice, inoffensive, superficial kitsch which seems blind to the pain of the world. I am reminded of William James's comments when he visited a supposedly idyllic resort in Chautauqua, New York, complete with evangelical preaching. He tells us of "the atrocious harmlessness of all things" and how he longed for the outside world, with its "heights and depths, the precipes and steep ideals, the gleams of the awful and the infinite."[20] Often I have been uplifted and inspired by the songs of the renewal movement, but, as I see it, too many betray an "atrocious harmlessness" which sadly lags behind the movement's increasing concern with contemporary social problems. Remarkably few songs deal with the common human experiences of failure, rejection, abandonment, protest, and alienation. (Contrast the Book of Psalms in the Old Testament!) And frequently the music also transmits a message of joy without tears, glory without suffering, resurrection without crucifixion. In James's words, we are missing

20. As quoted in William Edgar, *Taking Note of Music* (n.p.: SPCK, 1986), 18.

"gleams of the awful" along with the infinite. God did not simply rearrange the world into a satisfying pattern; He penetrated this sordid, broken, and distorted world as a man in order to transform and re-create it from within. The musician is summoned to follow in the footsteps of the Son of Man and to show that even out of despair a new beauty can be born. It would be absurd to suggest that, in order to bring glory to God, both these elements of honesty and hope need to be present in every piece of music. But occasionally they are combined within a single work. Is this not the case in Bach's Mass in B Minor, Mozart's *Requiem,* Messiaen's *L' Ascension,* Duke Ellington's *Come Sunday,* U2's song "Drowning Man?"

In this connection, we need to make a comment about judgment. I have said that God has not simply judged evil by wiping it out, but, through submitting to His own judgment on evil, has actually made it serve His purposes of love. God's judgment means setting right what has gone wrong. It never means simply writing off. This is vital for us to remember when it comes to assessing music. In Ruth Etchells' words, "Judging is discerning truly what is good and what is bad, and then putting it right."[21] Christian artists will not be helped by those who are waiting to pounce like hounds on some brand of music they find doctrinally suspect, and who then tear it apart under the pretext of preserving the "purity" of the gospel. There may be occasions when we may have to dismiss some music—particularly in the context of worship—as not

21. Dean and Porter, *Art in Question,* 67.

Jeremy Begbie

only sub- but actually anti-Christian, just as we need to take seriously the terrifying reality of hell and the real possibility of a final rejection from God's presence for those who spurn His love to the end. In a piece of music, there may be an implicit morality, for example, which is deeply offensive, perhaps even satanic. Most of us would draw the line with bands like Crass and the Dead Kennedys. But such instances are rare, and this kind of exclusion is not the heart of judgment in the Christian sense. Judgment is not the same as censorship. True Christian judgment should be trying to discover the larger world out of which the composer writes, the deep underlying patterns and principles which undergird and give a piece its coherence, and if criticism is necessary, pointing to a better way forward. Speaking as a musician who has often been battered in the name of "orthodoxy," I would like to think we have much to gain from a close look at the way in which God judges the world in Christ.

And so to our last theme: being drawn to Christ by the Spirit. Much has been written about "inspiration" in music, and Christians have not been slow to speak of "singing in the Spirit," "playing in the Spirit," "composing in the Spirit." It would be foolish to deny these claims outright, but if we are going to make any sense of the concept of inspiration we need to recall the close link in the New Testament between the Holy Spirit and Christ. Then we shall find that musical inspiration is not best thought of as a sort of divine takeover or possession, when a person suddenly becomes less than human. Nor is it some kind of guarantee which protects a composer from all criticism, as in: "the Spirit gave me this song today." (Who is going to disagree with the Spirit?) Rather, when a musician is inspired by the Spirit, he is transformed into the likeness of Christ, and through Christ enters into that active, responsive relationship with creation which was always intended for him, and through Christ is made more and more sensitive to the concerns, anxieties, and joys of others—his audience, his congregation, his public, and his fellow musicians, past and present. The test of an inspired church musician is not his ability to raise arms in ecstasy, or "show the choir who's boss," or play Widor's Toccata *prestissimo,* but whether he or she shows the marks of the crucified Savior.

CODA

To sum up, I have attempted to set music against the broad horizon of God's great acts of creation and redemption in order to discover more about its place in human life. The pervasive order of the world, which speaks of God's goodness, provides the basic setting in which the musician works. The contingence of the world reminds us of the hazard of idolizing music and the musician. God's faithful love towards creation as a whole removes any possible hesitancy we might have about being involved in an activity which is first and foremost

Jeremy Begbie

an interaction with the physical world. The musician's calling, as with any creative artist, is to discover, respect, and develop what he or she has received in creation, and to form out of the disorder of the world a richer order. All this is to be carried out with and for the sake of others. Above all, the musician finds his fulfillment as a priest of creation when he is bound to Christ by the Spirit, for in Him our humanity has been re-made and all creation been set right, and thus in Him the relation between the two healed and restored.

In closing, perhaps I can be bold enough to make some direct appeals. I would encourage *all* who read this to listen to as wide a variety of music as possible—the Renaissance motet and the Bob Dylan song, the Mahler symphony, and the Duke Ellington ballad. It is all too easy to get imprisoned in our private taste, fall into cultural laziness, and thus miss out on a wealth of music through which God might be waiting to enrich our lives.

I would hope that Christians with *political responsibility* would be thoroughly involved in the debate about the funding of the arts. Policies for government support of the arts carry with them an implicit view of the place of the arts in society. Judgments about quality are being made every day whether we acknowledge it or not, judgments which involve the allocation of public funds. Who are the arbiters of good taste? What are the criteria used to decide whether to back a particular composer or not? Financial gain? Is it not possible for the Christian to have a major impact in this arena?

I would entreat many more *theologians* to consider seriously how the arts might relate to the Christian faith. The paucity of contributions in this area is disappointing, to say the least. Much more influential than the professional theologians have been festivals like Greenbelt, through which many Christians have been made to think as never before about the place of the arts in their faith, and bodies such as the Arts Centre Group in London, where professional Christian artists can meet and talk over issues confronting them in their work. The world of theology and the world of the arts have much to learn from each other, but more bridges need to be built if any effective dialogue is to take place.

I would hope that *church leaders* would do more to encourage the musicians in their congregations. As Tony Jasper points out, "It is not unusual for the Christian artist who believes that the gospel is about creating a community of caring and nurturing people (which in essence it is) to find in developing his artistic endeavors that he meets with lack of interest, or even distaste and hostility."[22] Lucky the Christian musician who has encouragement from somebody experienced and perceptive (as well as honest). Unlucky the person confronted by armchair detractors with their evangelical checklists. Musicians need space to experiment, room to explore, and even leeway to make mistakes.

Finally I would make a plea that *Christian musicians* learn more about what it means to transform their culture.

22. Tony Jasper, *Jesus and the Christian in a Pop Culture* (n.p.: Royce, 1984), 76.

Christian musicians cannot afford to retreat into a ghetto of the like-minded. Perhaps more than ever before, we need people with a vision to venture out, learn the musical styles of our modern culture, and remold them into something richer. As John Berger has stressed, it is the function of the truly original artist to renew the tradition to which he belongs.[23] The composers of Negro spirituals have much to teach us in this respect. They took Puritan hymns, baroque dance suites, West African tribal rhythms, and allowed the gospel to weld that extraordinary diversity into a unique musical form, one which genuinely expressed the faith and convictions of the slave community. It was that remarkable combination which gave rise to a whole stream of musical culture—blues, jazz, pop, and rock—which has radically reshaped music in the twentieth century. Could it be that somewhere we are on the eve of a similar breakthrough today?

23. John Berger, *Permanent Red* (n.p.: Methuen, 1960), 104.

Appendix

BOOKS AND PRINTED RESOURCES FOR THE MUSICIAN

MIX Bookshelf
Catalog of books on all aspects of music and the music industry. If it's in book form, it probably is available here.
c/o Whitehurst and Clark, Inc., 100 Newfield Ave., Edison, NJ 08837. Toll-Free U.S. & Canada (800) 233-9604

All You Need to Know About the Music Business
by Donald S. Passman. A very comprehensive overview of all aspects of the business side of music. If you're serious about recording and touring, read this first!
Simon & Schuster • ISBN 0-671-88304-6 • $25.00

The Responsibility of the Christian Musician
by Glenn Kaiser. A look at the Christian musician's responsibility to God, to family, to the Church, and to those whom she or he affects with her or his ministry. Crucial information from a veteran of contemporary Christian music.
Cornerstone Press Chicago • ISBN 0-940895-22-6 • $7.95

RESOURCES MENTIONED IN
MORE LIKE THE MASTER

Reality
P.O. Box 1562, Paraparaumu Beach 6450, New Zealand

Cornerstone
939 W. Wilson, Ave., Chicago, IL 60640

CrossRhythms
P.O. Box 183, Plymouth PL3 4YN England

Art House
P.O. Box 210694, Nashville,TN 37221

CCM
107 Kenner Ave., Nashville, TN 37205

Prism *(the official publication of Evangelicals for Social Action)*
10 Lancaster Ave., Wynnewood, PA 19096

True Tunes News
210 W. Front St., Wheaton, IL 60187

OTHER PUBLICATIONS

Release
402 BNA Drive, Ste. 508, Bldg 100, Nashville, TN 37217

7 Ball
402 BNA Drive, Ste. 508, Bldg 100, Nashville, TN 37217

HM
6614 Bradley Dr., Austin, TX 78723

Christianity & The Arts
P.O. Box 118088, Chicago, IL 60611

ORGANIZATIONS WORKING WITH MUSICIANS AND THE ARTS

ASCAP
One Lincoln Plaza, New York, NY 10023
(212) 621-6000, E-mail: info@ascap.com

Bay Area Christian Artist's Network
512 Haddon Rd., Oakland, CA 94606

BMI
320 West 57th Street, New York, NY 10019, (212) 586-2000

10 Music Square East, Nashville, TN 37203, (615) 401-2000

8730 Sunset Blvd., 3rd Flr. West, Los Angeles, CA 90069
(310) 657-6947

Center for Arts & Religion
Wesley Theological Seminary, 4500 Massachusetts Ave. NW,
Washington, DC 20016

Center for Liturgy & the Arts
4327 Ravensworth Rd. #210, Annandale, VA 22003

Christians in the Arts Networking (CAN)
9 Westminster Ave., Arlington, MA 02174-0003

Christians in the Visual Arts
P.O. Box 18117, Minneapolis, MN 55418-0017

Institute for Theology & the Arts
P.O. Box 379, Paddington 2021, NSW, Australia

CHRISTIAN MUSICIANS ON THE INTERNET[1]

The Art House

http://www.netcentral.net/arthouse

Access the Art House resource base, the text of all Art House newsletters, full transcripts and outlines of selected lectures from various Art House events, and a complete schedule of all Art House functions.

Christian Artists List

http://linus.cs.ohio.edu/~wlhd/alight/cartists.html

If there's information available on your favorite Christian musician, chances are you'll find it here.

---

1. From "The Christian Arts on the Net," by Nick Barré reprinted from the Art House newsletter, Spring 1996

Christian Music Web Sites
http://linus.cs.ohio.edu/~wlhd/alight/cmusic.html
This site links to Christian music organizations around the globe.

Cornerstone Festival
http://www.mcs.net/~patp/festmain.html
Up-to-date news on the music and arts festival sponcored by Jesus People USA.

NetCentral
http://www.netcentral.net
Many Christian music sites are located here.

OTHER INTERNET SITES OF INTEREST

Christian Classics Ethereal Library
http://www.cs.pitt.edu/~planting/books/
Download entire books by such Christian thinkers as Milton, Bunyan, Augustine, Calvin, and Chesterton.

Christian Resource List
http://saturn.colorado.edu.8080/Christian/list.html
A great collection of Christian links organized by topics! (This is a great place to use as a launching pad to find other Christian sites.)

Gospel Communications Network

http://www.gospelcom.net/

Several important Christian organizations are located here, including Ligonier Ministries, Navigators Ministries, InterVarsity Christian Fellowship, Gospel Films, and Youth Specialties.

McKenzie Study Center

http://www.efn.org/~mscenter/

This ministry, based in Eugene, Oregon, has an excellent collection of essays on the arts. Writers include Jeff Johnson, R. Wesley Hurd, and Ron Julian.

Index

PSALMS, HYMNS AND SPIRITUAL SONGS
Donald Thiessen

The perfect reference book for worship leaders, music students and teachers, and musicians who want to develop a biblically based philosophy about music and its place in the Church. *Psalms* contains all the verses in the Bible that mention music—over 450 verses! Designed for quick searches as well as in-depth studies, with topical subheads, contextual references, and detailed index.
ISBN 0-940895-06-4 • $6.95

THE RESPONSIBILITY OF THE CHRISTIAN MUSICIAN
Glenn Kaiser

A no-nonsense look at the musician's life from a Christian music veteran.

> "Your book is a welcome contribution to a vocational calling in which there seems to be too little thinking, accountability, and humility."

—SCOTTY SMITH, pastor, Christ Community Church, Nashville
ISBN 0-940895-22-6 • $7.95

ALL MY DAYS: SONGS OF WORSHIP & WITNESS
Glenn Kaiser

A companion songbook to the celebrated recording, *All My Days.* Gives the small group or church worship leader full access to the lyrics, chords, and melodies for all the songs.
ISBN 0-940895-16-1 • $7.95

LET THE WHOLE WORLD SING
Corean Bakke

A great book for music leaders. Many churches today are seeking the need for a multicultural worship program. Corean Bakke gives a step-by-step account of how she assembled an international worship team and organized a diverse multicultural program. The book includes the hymnal, *Aleluya,* featuring fifty-seven worship songs from seventeen different countries.
ISBN 0-940895-18-8 • $13.00

ALELUYA
Corean Bakke & Tony Payne

Aleluya brings the songs of Lausanne II together again, re-type-set, with an easy-to-use lay-flat wire binding. All songs appear in their original language (not transliterations), with an accompanying English translation. This is the perfect resource for church musicologists, and works very well for missions and cross-cultural events. Fifty-seven songs from seventeen countries included.

ISBN 0-940895-20-X • $5.00

CORNERSTONE PRESS CHICAGO BOOK ORDER FORM

CORNERSTONE PRESS CHICAGO
939 W. Wilson Ave., Suite 202C • Chicago, IL 60640

TITLE	QTY.	AMOUNT

Shipping—$3.00 for first book, $.70 for each additional book (shipped U.S. Postal Service book rate. Allow 3-5 weeks for processing and delivery). Foreign orders—please contact us for air and surface rates. All orders outside the U.S. must be prepaid by money order of U.S. currency.

SUBTOTAL	
SHIPPING	
TOTAL	

NAME _____

ADDRESS _____

CITY _____ STATE _____ ZIP _____

❏ MasterCard ❏ VISA ❏ Check/Money Order Enclosed (U.S. funds only)

Credit card number _____ Exp. date _____

Signature _____ Telephone number _____